Accused

For Elizabeth, Alfred, Efi, William,
and a much beloved Goblin.

Accused

British Witches
Throughout History

Willow Winsham

PEN & SWORD
HISTORY

First published in Great Britain in 2016 and reprinted in this format
in 2022 and 2024 by
Pen & Sword History
an imprint of
Pen & Sword Books Ltd
47 Church Street
Barnsley
South Yorkshire
S70 2AS

ISBN 978 1 39901 453 3

A CIP catalogue record for this book is available from the British
Library

Typeset in Ehrhardt by
Mac Style Ltd, Bridlington, East Yorkshire
Printed in the UK on paper from a sustainable source by CPI
Group (UK) Ltd, Croydon, CR0 4YY

Pen & Sword Books Ltd incorporates the imprints of Pen & Sword
Archaeology, Atlas, Aviation, Battleground, Discovery, Family
History, History, Maritime, Military, Naval, Politics, Railways,
Select, Transport, True Crime, and Fiction, Frontline Books, Leo
Cooper, Praetorian Press, Seaforth Publishing and Wharncliffe.

For a complete list of Pen & Sword titles please contact
PEN & SWORD BOOKS LIMITED
47 Church Street, Barnsley, South Yorkshire, S70 2AS, England
E-mail: enquiries@pen-and-sword.co.uk
Website: www.pen-and-sword.co.uk

Contents

Acknowledgements

These acknowledgements might mark the start of the book, but they were actually the part that was written last. Over the last few months, there have been times when I didn't think I would make it to this point at all, but the support and encouragement of so many truly wonderful people has seen me through.

In light of that I would like to thank the following people. Firstly, Kate Bohdanowicz for suggesting I submit a proposal for the book in the first place, as without her encouragement I wouldn't have ever thought to do so. Emma Toulson, who read and critiqued my submission chapter (and many more throughout) and has helped make this a better book. My long-suffering husband who has been wonderful throughout, both in practical help and listening to me rant and rave about the entire process, and my two children who have been remarkably accepting of the fact that 'mummy needs to do some work now' and have even shown an interest in what I'm writing. Catherine Curzon for innumerable instances of help and general all-round moral support. My parents, because without them I wouldn't be the person I am today. Sarah and Jako Van der Walt for letting me go on about all things witchy and for helping get an author photo that I don't actually hate. Debbie Corlett and Tabitha Luddem-Lounds for reading through the whole thing when I couldn't stand to look at it anymore and for many helpful suggestions that have led to the text that you are about to read.

I'd also like to say a general thank you to all the friends who have patiently listened to me explaining the finer points of witchcraft history or talking about people turning into cats, but especially to Sally Collins who helps me keep things in perspective and enjoys a good and much needed giggle. And last but by no means least, An Victoir, for being the best 'Goblin' that I could hope to have known, and without whom I would have given up writing long before the opportunity came to write this book.

There have also been a number of very lovely organisations and individuals who have provided invaluable help with research, images and permissions and I would like to thank: Derbyshire Record Office, Hertfordshire Archives and Local Studies, Bedfordshire and Luton Archives and Records Service, Ipswich Record Office, Bury St Edmunds Record Office, Llyfrgell Genedlaethol Cymru/The National Library of Wales, Lincolnshire Archives, Devon Archives and Local Studies Service, Ilkeston Library, The British Library, David Newman, Bev Plumbley, Ted Rayson, Neil Deans, Bill Church, Alan Stewart, Mark Evans from Quickfire Media, The HMS Barham Association, Stephen Flinders, Gillian Kenny, Tracy Borman, Richard Suggett, Malcolm Gaskill, Hugh Ryan, Nicky Flynn, Jennifer Mortensen and anyone else who has contributed their time and expertise to this project.

And of course finally a heartfelt thanks to the good people at Pen and Sword who believed this book was worth writing.

The entire project has been a learning curve and a half, and it might be a cliché, but I truly mean it when I say that I hope people enjoy reading it as much as I enjoyed writing it.

List of Illustrations

Tomb of Bishop Ledrede (*By kind permission of St Canice's Cathedral, Kilkenny*)

The Kyteler Slab. (*By kind permission of St Canice's Cathedral, Kilkenny*)

Kyteler's Inn, Kilkenny. (*By kind permission of Nicky Flynn*)

Illustration of witches with their familiars. (© *Wellcome Library, London*)

Mill Pond, Milton Ernest. (*By kind permission of David Newman and Bev Plumbley*)

The Swimming of a Witch (© *Wellcome Library, London*)

Indictments against Gwen ferch Ellis (*By permission of Llyfrgell Genedlaethol Cymru / The National Library of Wales*)

Guilty verdict against Gwen ferch Ellis with sentence of hanging. (*By permission of Llyfrgell Genedlaethol Cymru / The National Library of Wales*)

Tomb inscription for Francis Manners, 6th Earl of Rutland (© *Ted Rayson*)

Detail from Rutland tomb, showing Henry and Francis Manners (© *Quickfire Media*)

Witch's Cottage, Bottesford. (© *Ted Rayson*)

Matthew Hopkins, Witchfinder general, with two supposed witches calling out the names of their demons, some of which are represented by animals. (© Wellcome Library, London.)

Quarter Sessions document Q/SB/2/170 dctailing information against Anne Wagg. (*By permission of Derbyshire Record Office*)

St Mary's Church, Ilkeston.

Witches and Devils dancing. (© *Wellcome Library, London*)

A White Faced Witch and a Black Faced Witch. (© *Wellcome Library, London*)

A Devil and a Witch Making a Nail. (© *Wellcome Library, London*)

A Witch at her cauldron Surrounded by Beasts. Etching by J. van de Velde II, 1626 (© *Wellcome Library, London*)

Permissions

The True Informer, (23 July 1645) (© *The British Library Board, E.67–80.314–327*)

Cotta, John *A Short Discoverie of the Unobserved Dangers* (London 1612) (© *The British Library Board, 551.a.2.(1.)*)

Composer's Notes, *The Confession of Isobel Gowdie* (1990) (© *Copyright by James MacMillan*)

Bragge, Francis, *A Defence of the Proceedings against Jane Wenham*, (*London, 1712*) (©*The British Library Board, 8630.ee.17*)

Bragge, Francis, *A Full and Impartial Account of the Discovery of Sorcery and Witchcraft, Practis'd by Jane Wenham of Walkern*, (London, 1712) (©*The British Library Board, 8630.bb.18*)

Bragge, Francis, *Witchcraft Farther Display'd* (London, 1712) (© *The British Library Board, 8631.aaa.42*)

Hutchinson, Francis, *A Historical Essay Concerning Witchcraft* (*London, 1718*) (© *The British Library Board, 719.h.13*)

The Case of the Hertfordshire Witchcraft Consider'd (London, 1712) (© *The British Library Board, 1417.i.38*)

Exeter and Plymouth Gazette for 13 March, 1852. (© *The British Newspaper Archive (www.britishnewspaperarchive.co.uk*)

Exeter and Plymouth Gazette, 24 April 1852. (© *The British Newspaper Archive*)

North Devon Journal, 29 April, 1852. (© *The British Newspaper Archive*)

Supplement to the Western Times, Exeter, July 14, 1860. (© *The British Newspaper Archive*)

Taunton Courier, and Western Advertiser, 18 July, 1860. (© *The British Newspaper Archive*)

Exeter and Plymouth Gazette, 6 October, 1860. (© *The British Newspaper Archive*)

A brief note on spelling. For ease of reading, the majority of spellings have been standardised and modernised throughout the text.

Introduction: The World of the Accused

There shall not be found among you any one that maketh his son or his daughter to pass through the fire, or that useth divination, or an observer of times, or an enchanter, or a witch, Or a charmer, or a consulter with familiar spirits, or a wizard, or a necromancer. For all that do these things are an abomination unto the LORD: and because of these abominations the LORD thy God doth drive them out from before thee.

Deuteronomy 18:10–18:12

This is a book about witches, eleven witches to be exact, picked from across the centuries of the history of the British Isles.

Witches have been consistently feared, revered, sought after and persecuted throughout history. The evil within, made all the more insidious because she – or he – looked just like anyone else; a witch could kill your cattle, destroy your livelihood and endanger your loved ones through the invisible means of spells, evil spirits or through a touch or a look. There were ways to identify witches, but these were by no means fool-proof. Ultimately, the witch could be anyone – a neighbour, a wife, a friend – and it was this very fact that made them so dangerous. If anyone could be a witch, then literally everyone was suspect. It is not hard, in these circumstances, to understand why people were accused of what became the most terrible of crimes.

The 'accused' covered in this book are all women with a story that demands to be told. Men were also accused of being witches but at least eighty-five per cent of those accused and prosecuted for witchcraft were women, and the majority of accusers were likewise female. These accusations were made in the everyday, humdrum, ebb and flow of community life, in small communities and across families, with outcomes that were devastating and, often, deadly.

Comprehensive figures for witchcraft executions are, at best, only an estimate. The records of the time were often incomplete or have simply not survived for today's researchers. The best modern estimates of the total executed for witchcraft across Europe rest between 40,000 and 50,000.[1] Within the British Isles it is believed that in England around 200 people were executed for the crime, whilst in Wales and Ireland the numbers are significantly lower. Scotland trumps all however with a shade over 3,800 people accused and, at a very rough estimate, some 2,500 of these found guilty and executed.[2] The full figures for those accused of witchcraft, including those acquitted or those found guilty and suffered to live, cannot be truly known. Nevertheless, we can be certain that not everyone accused was found guilty and not all those found guilty were executed, thus presenting a wide range of experiences and outcomes.

Whatever the result of an accusation, guilty or innocent, to be accused of being a witch was a life-changing experience, through which reputation, friends, family, and life itself could be lost. Crucial to an understanding of the stories that follow is that belief in religion and magic was strong for the major part of the history of the British Isles. The Devil was believed to exist in a very real sense; as did the need to protect and distance oneself and one's family from the danger of entanglement with the forces of darkness. The witch herself, capable of performing spells and charms that could either harm or help, became the reification of this; a physical representation that must be protected against or eradicated. Combined with the unpredictable occurrences of life and death, this meant witches were seen as a very real threat and the process of being accused of witchcraft was often deadly – either through legal execution or the outpouring of popular justice.

It was not until the 1500s that the first concerted action was taken against witchcraft through the courts by legislation. Henry VIII was the first to class witchcraft as a felony in 1542, though this was swiftly repealed in 1547 by his son, Edward VI, and it was not until 1563 that witchcraft again returned to the statute books. From then until 1736, with some changes in 1604, it was possible to prosecute and, if warranted, execute someone accused of being a witch. In 1736 the law was changed to reflect the Enlightenment notion that witchcraft was a relic of a superstitious past, and thus criminalised the *belief* in witchcraft. Despite this change on paper however, there was little change in the outlook of the population at large, who remained convinced of the danger of witches and were resistant to the idea that witchcraft was no longer a threat. Indeed, in some areas, suspected witches were still being accused and attacked well into the twentieth century, with some cases still lingering within living memory.

Whilst this book is many things, it is not is an in-depth discussion of the theory or historiography of witchcraft as there already exist many excellent works covering these areas. In these, individual cases are often used to illustrate themes and trends when presenting research on witchcraft in history, but this study will use the themes and ideas to illustrate and illuminate the individuals behind them. From our contemporary perspective it is impossible to accurately reconstruct a complete picture of any of these women; we can only catch glimpses of what they looked like, sounded like, how it felt to be in their presence. However, it is through these glimpses, furtive and fleeting, that we are able to gain an insight into their experience, to discover their circumstances and just what it was that led them to their unenviable fates.

By turns unbelievable, amusing and outright terrifying, the journey through their stories is about to begin. Suspend your disbelief, step back in time, and prepare to enter the world of the accused.

Chapter One

The Irish Sorceress: Alice Kyteler (1324)

'And although in their unholy art she was mistress of the ritual she was nothing, she said, in comparison with her mistress, from whom she had learnt all those things and many others. In fact there was no-one in the kingdom of England more skilled ... nor did she think there was anyone in the world her equal in the art of witchcraft.'

Confession of Petronilla de Meath, 1324

Ruled by the English, invaded by the Scots, and struck by the famine that affected the whole of Europe, Ireland during the early fourteenth century had seen much turmoil and unrest. By the time the first quarter of the century was coming to a close however, things were looking up, and more peaceful times were hoped for by all.[1]

The prosperous Southern-Irish town of Kilkenny was no exception to this turbulent existence; granted a charter by William Marshall in 1207, the town marked the seat of the Bishops of Ossory and, like the rest of Ireland, looked forward to the end of years of upheaval. Kilkenny would have to wait a little longer for peace however, as in 1324 events were to unfold that would shake the town, and the very diocese, to the core.

From a prosperous Flemish merchant family, and with four husbands to her name, Alice Kyteler was a woman of wealth and connections. She and her money-lending son, William Outlawe, were much admired and envied throughout Kilkenny, so it is not surprising that, sooner or later, scandal would attach itself to her name – with devastating consequences.

Alice, it was said, was a witch. Guilty of bewitching four men into loving and marrying her she had then hastened them to their untimely ends. Not only that, but she had used her sorcery to persuade each man to leave the majority of their wealth to her, depriving her reluctant step-children of what, they felt, was duly theirs.[2] Utterly convinced of this, at some point prior to 1324, the children of Alice's second and third husbands had initiated proceedings against their step-mother. It was not an uncommon tale of familial jealousies, but one that would take on a whole new significance in the presence of Richard Ledrede, Bishop of Ossory, to whom they made their complaint.

Since his arrival in Ireland in 1317, Ledrede had been a man on a mission.[3] Intent on tackling the ever present threat of heresy and determined that the towns under his protection would be free from the vices that plagued the rest of the country, it was with great consternation that he learnt a group of heretics had been practising with impunity in Kilkenny. At the head of this group was alleged to be none other than Dame Alice Kyteler.

There were seven charges made against Alice and her accomplices, encompassing heresy, sorcery and poisoning. Damning indeed, but when the bishop wrote to Roger Outlawe, the Lord Chancellor of Ireland, with the purpose of arresting Alice and her associates, he found his way blocked by the efforts of Alice and her influential contacts.[4] Unimpressed by Ledrede's petition, the chancellor and the seneschal of Kilkenny, Lord Arnold le Poer, contacted the bishop to express their displeasure, insisting that he desist immediately from his endeavours to prosecute Alice.[5] Not one for half measures where matters of the faith were concerned, Ledrede reported that he would do no such thing and thus began a feud that was to go back and forth for months.

The chancellor, no doubt irked at this tenacity and hoping Ledrede would drop the matter if enough obstacles were set in his way, declared that he would only issue a warrant for Alice's arrest once a public investigation had been carried out. Not only that, the suspects had to be excommunicated – cast out from the favour and protection of the church – for a period of forty days.

Unhappy in his turn with the way the secular authorities were dealing with his concerns, Ledrede took matters into his own hands and summoned Alice to appear before him. However, when those serving the citation arrived at her son's house (where she had been staying), Alice was nowhere to be found. Unperturbed, on the day Alice was supposed to appear before him, Ledrede went ahead and excommunicated her in her absence. Angry that Alice had evaded him, he went further still and turned his attention to her son. William Outlawe was ordered to appear before the bishop on a specified date, charged not only with heresy, but also protecting and giving shelter to heretics, including his own mother and those in her household.

Furious, Lord Arnold visited Ledrede at the nearby Priory of Kells, where he 'pleaded most passionately' with the bishop to cease his quest.[6] Although the interview lasted until midnight, his words had little effect and finally, the exasperated seneschal resorted to insults and abuse in an attempt to get what he wanted. When this still had no effect, Arnold, in a final show of power, had Ledrede arrested the next morning on the outskirts of the town.

There was little Ledrede could do to resist. He nevertheless prolonged the matter for as long as possible, reading through the document that ordered his arrest and displaying the seal of the seneschal so the gathering crowd could be in no doubt as to who had ordered the arrest of their bishop. After great display, Ledrede finally went with his captors, pausing yet again at the prison gates where he told his distraught household that they should not weep, but instead be glad because his unfair treatment would be honour in the eyes of God.[7]

Ledrede was incarcerated in Kilkenny Castle where, with no doubt as to the righteousness of his cause, he played the wronged martyr to Lord Arnold's secular might. Although Arnold might be seen to have the upper hand the Bishop gained much support during this time. He also had a deadly ace up his sleeve; Ledrede placed the entire diocese under interdict, removing any offices that the church would usually perform from all who lived there. No burials, baptisms or other rituals were to be carried out, leaving in mortal danger the souls of the wealthy and the poor alike.

With the two powers locked in stalemate the date that William Outlawe had been cited to appear came and went, as Arnold had no doubt intended. The purpose of his imprisonment served, Ledrede was released to welcoming crowds seventeen days later, with the hope that the interdict would be lifted and the matter regarding Alice would at last be dropped.

It soon became clear however, that the bishop's determination to see Alice and her associates brought to justice had not cooled. On the contrary, he again summoned Alice and her son to answer the serious charges against them. In a somewhat unlikely coincidence, Ledrede received a summons of his own, demanding his presence in Dublin to answer for placing his diocese under interdict – on the exact same day that Alice and William were due to appear before the bishop.[8]

Alice had not been idle through this, using her lawyers to file counter-charges of defamation against Ledrede in Dublin, declaring the excommunication invalid due to her absence and seeking redress for this unfairness. Ledrede argued that Alice had in fact been convicted in person (though how and when is unclear as she had not attended the previous summons) then declared that she was guilty of relapse into heresy – a crime that was indisputably punishable by death.

Despite this, Alice was set free to go about the town as she wished. She made good use of this advantage, cultivating the friendship of the mayor, William Doucemanne, and was wined and dined by the most influential in the town. Whether she was fearful or angry we can only speculate, but one thing was certain; Alice Kyteler was not going to submit quietly, bishop or no bishop.

The result of these machinations was a second summons to Dublin for Ledrede; upon arrival however, he found that the court assembled there was set firmly against him. The following day, Arnold produced a document that came from the King in England, discussing the power of the church. The forthright seneschal declared his opinion on the subject, announcing that 'if some tramp from England or somewhere has obtained his bull or privilege in the pope's court, we don't have to obey that bull unless it has been enjoined on us by the king's seal.'[9] Arnold and the bishop thus entered into a lively debate, which again deteriorated into angry words from the seneschal and resulted in him storming from the building. With no sign of a rapprochement in sight it was eventually decided that outside mediation was needed and four bishops were chosen to hear the argument with both Ledrede and Arnold given the chance to air their grievances. Finally an uneasy truce was reached, with the bishop magnanimously declaring that he would forgive Lord Arnold the wrongs done against him if the seneschal would not protect known heretics and would allow Ledrede to continue his work against the enemies of the church. To seal the deal, the two men exchanged an embrace and a kiss before the assembled bishops and councillors, with all concerned hoping the matter was now at an end.

Despite this, it was not long before hostilities were resumed once again. Ledrede would not cease in his dogged determination to see the heretical

Alice and her son brought to justice and, whilst in Dublin, sent officials to Kilkenny to enquire as to the practices of the heretics – where he was swiftly thwarted by the seneschal.[10] One party at least had grown weary of the game by this point and Arnold also organised an inquisition himself into the matter of heresy in the area, intending to clear Alice's name once and for all.

The outcome was unexpected and disastrous. Instead of proving Alice's innocence, the citizens of Kilkenny firmly and publicly came forward with evidence that spoke all too clearly of her guilt; the allegations against Alice and her associates were serious indeed.

It was claimed that by denying Christ and abstaining from partaking in the sacraments of the Church, Alice and her followers could count on being granted whatever they wanted.[11] As if this were not bad enough, it was believed that these heretics went further still in their contempt, appropriating some of the rituals of the church for their own nefarious ends. In one such example, Alice and her friends were alleged to have excommunicated those they disliked; no one was safe from their ire, with even their own husbands being targeted in such a fashion if they caused the group displeasure.

Not only that, but they were said to make sacrifices to demons using living animals, meeting at the crossroads to carry out these gruesome rituals. Once the sacrifice had taken place, Alice and her fellow heretics would supposedly ask the demons they summoned for answers to their questions and help in carrying out their business. Whilst performing their perverted versions of the church sacraments, those involved were said to make potions from the intestines of the previously sacrificed animals, casting spells that could cause harm to their enemies or influence their emotions in any way that took their fancy.

On one fact in particular, those who came forward were unequivocal: Alice was the leader of the group, the most dangerous of them all. It was well-known that she had a particular demon who came only to her, going by the name of Robin, son of Art.[12] Along with using the demon to do her will, Alice also took him into her bed, completing the list of horrifying practices attributed to her name. Added to the accusations from her step-children that she had bewitched their fathers to death, the evidence against her was now greater than even the seneschal could ignore.

With no choice but to act, Arnold had his sheriffs arrest only the poorer women out of those accused, their lack of money and influence leaving them powerless to protest. Wealth and influence stood in Alice's stead however and she was openly allowed to escape, fleeing the country with the daughter of her maidservant, Petronilla de Meath who had been arrested along with the others.

Cheated of his prey, Ledrede turned again on William Outlawe. Alice's son was charged with heresy and the aiding and abetting of heretics, to which he duly confessed on bended knee.[13] After a short incarceration in the castle, William was released on bail; far from carrying out his penance he continued to shelter heretics, keeping some under his own roof, before being re-arrested, and chained in irons.

Alice's maid-servant Petronilla was not as fortunate as her well-connected mistress. On Ledrede's orders, she was whipped, or beaten, six times and confessed to everything required of her, damning her mistress in the process.[14] Alice had, Petronilla was clear, been the leader and instigator of everything they had done and there was none more powerful or better versed in sorcery than her mistress in Ireland and England, or perhaps even the world. Penance was offered to Petronilla, but she did not accept it, and, refusing to repent, was burnt on 3rd November 1324 before a large watching crowd.[15]

Nothing further is known of Alice Kyteler or her whereabouts.[16] Where and how she lived out her days and what assumed identity she took on to conceal herself from discovery can, unfortunately, only be met with guesswork and outright speculation. One thing of which we can be certain, however, is that whatever fate befell her, it is unlikely to have been worse than that which awaited her in Ireland.

That there were tensions between Alice and the residents of Kilkenny before the drama of 1324 is evident. One telling event occurred in 1303, when a raid on William Outlawe's house revealed the not insignificant sum of £3,000 hidden away. When questioned, Outlawe stated that it belonged to his mother Alice, and her then husband, Adam le Blund. William Outlawe went on to complain that the money had been taken by those who had unearthed it, along with £100 of his own money. It seems there was an ulterior motive at play: Alice and her husband claimed that those who had taken the money had made false charges against them in order that it be declared forfeit and not returned to them. In a precursor to the later allegations against Alice, it was said that the couple had killed her first husband so that they could seize his wealth and then marry.[17] Alice, le Blund, and a Rose Outlawe, possibly a daughter from Alice's first marriage or a relation of her first husband, were taken to Kilkenny where they faced the threat of execution. They were freed however, when sureties were provided by John le Poer, the man who would become Alice's fourth and final husband.[18]

It was clear that there was a long-burning jealousy and resentment of Alice and her son. Alice's second husband, Adam le Blund, had left all his possessions to William Outlawe when he died, despite having children of his own from a previous marriage. It is worth noting that eventually, John le Poer also became convinced of Alice's intent to kill him through harmful magic. One day, despite his ill state, he grabbed the keys to his wife's storage chests from her and discovered a selection of gruesome ingredients that confirmed his suspicions.[19]

It is tempting to view Alice's story through the lens of the later English and Continental witch-hunt, but this case was unique for several reasons. Significantly, the burning of Petronilla de Meath marked the first recorded burning of a woman for heresy in Ireland. Not only that, but Alice's case happened before the passing of any formal witchcraft legislation in Ireland and was the first recorded case where the charges of heresy and witchcraft were combined.

Another important detail that makes the case stand out is the reference to demon worship, because it is one of only three allegations of deliberate devil-worship on record for the period.[20] The reference to the sexual relationship between a witch and the Devil is also striking, as the belief that Alice slept with her demon marks the first known instance of such an accusation in Europe.[21] The idea would later become a main feature of witchcraft accusations and confessions on the Continent, but never became standard in English cases.

Also of interest in the charges against Alice were those involving spells and rituals. Using the conveniently acquired skull of a robber who had been decapitated (presumably in punishment) as a vessel, Alice and her associates cooked the innards of the cocks that they had sacrificed at the crossroads. As if that were not enough, worms, herbs, and various other trimmings such as nails and hair from baby boys who had died before being baptised were mixed into this already unpleasant concoction. Despite the gruesome nature of the mixtures however, it is suggested that these were not all intended for harm, with Petronilla confessing that she and her mistress had made 'concoctions, lotions and powders' for a variety of purposes.[22] One of the ingredients mentioned is milfoil, a herb used both medicinally and to treat wounds.[23] Body parts were used in magic to influence the emotions, which supports the mention of love magic in the accusations against Alice.[24] The scorpions and spiders mentioned in Alice's potions however, suggest a less innocent purpose, and it seems that the magic said to be performed by Alice and her associates varied depending on what they needed to accomplish.

The main source of evidence for the case and Alice's life in general is *A Contemporary Narrative of the Proceedings Against Dame Alice Kyteler Prosecuted for Sorcery in 1324,* a document that was probably written by Ledrede or one of his supporters. A Franciscan trained in France, Ledrede's time at the Papal court in Avignon meant that he would be familiar with the increasing hostility there towards magic and magical practitioners. Whilst his experience would better place him for rooting out heresy, it would also crucially colour his perceptions and lead him to ask the kind of questions that would produce the responses he expected to find.[25]

Alice has been portrayed as many things over the years: an evil sorceress; a temptress; a gold-digger or a victim of the battle between Church and State. Indeed, as a wealthy, independent woman, she was both powerful and vulnerable. Through a series of strategic marriages, Alice had added to her own inherited wealth and prestige but this had also created discord and resentment both within the families of her husbands and in society. There is no evidence as to whether her marriages were successful in terms of love and companionship, but the result of either luck or management meant Alice was a wealthy woman indeed. It was also apparent that tensions were just waiting to bubble over.

Given Alice's number of marriages it has been suggested that she must have been decidedly attractive.[26] This is entirely speculative, as there is no surviving portrait or description of Alice to shed light on her physical appearance. Whatever her looks, it was clear that her personality and abilities made her a formidable woman who commanded both respect and fear.

It is unknown when the Kyteler family first arrived in Ireland, but there is a stone that now rests in St Canice's Cathedral in Kilkenny to the memory of a Josef Kyteler. His death is recorded as taking place in 1280, indicating that the family were established in the town by that time.[27] The stone has been dated to the late-thirteenth century, and was discovered in High Street in Kilkenny in 1894 during the renovation of a building that now houses the newspaper office of the *Kilkenny People*.[28] At the time it was the oldest date-inscribed tomb to be found in Kilkenny.[29] The discovery of bones in the area and signs of doors and windows of an ecclesiastical structure, along with the tombs (a couple of others were found across the street) indicates that this was the site of a very early burial ground.[30] In an ironic twist of fate, Archbishop Ledrede also found his final resting place at St Canice's. This stalwart nemesis of Alice and her son died in 1360 after a chequered and turbulent life; ultimately he had the final victory, dying while still in office despite having had it removed from him several times.

A building generally believed to have been Alice's former residence is Kilkenny's popular Kyteler's Inn. A building named 'Kettlers Inne' was recorded on the site from at least 1639, at which time it is referred to as having been 'anciently' known by that name, implying that it had been present for a good time before that.[31] The inn is described as neighbouring Kyran's Well, and it is said that this would put it at the northern end of King Street. During Alice's time it would have been a place for locals to meet and drink together, with the modern sense of providing lodgings for visitors only coming into use after the monasteries, which usually performed that purpose, were suppressed in the mid-sixteenth century.[32] It is mentioned that the name, corrupted into Kelter, was still present in the area at the time the piece was written in 1862. Today there are a couple of instances of that name in Ireland, but Kyteler, Outlawe and variants seem to have been lost.

The myth of Alice Kyteler continued to grow long after she fled Ireland. Although absent from the near-contemporary records of *The Narrative* and the records kept by John Clyn, a friar from Kilkenny, there are several 'facts' that have crept into accounts of Alice over the years and which now make up part of her enduring memory. One oft repeated addition is recorded in James Grace's *Annales Hiberniae*; that Alice would sweep all the dust and dirt of the street towards the house of her son, William, declaring as she did so 'may all the luck of Kilkenny come to this house.'[33] Another was that she kept in her possession an ointment that she would rub onto a beam that would then enable her and her associates to fly to their devilish gatherings.[34] Other additions include the 'facts' that Alice was guilty of sacrificing nine cocks, that she owned a communion host with the name of the Devil on it, and that before she was burned, Petronilla de Meath had accused William Outlawe of being as, if not more, guilty than Alice was.[35] These supposed 'facts' are unsubstantiated, and some at least can be taken as a reflection of ideas that later developed around witchcraft, such as witches flying to the Sabbat. Fabricated as these later additions probably are, they are useful in tracing the growth and development of the myth of Alice, appropriated by each generation to fill a need or in an attempt at understanding, her reputation across the years interpreted in the light of the society examining her.[36]

The lack of detail regarding large parts of Alice's life has given plenty of scope for speculation and interpretation. W.B. Yeats captured her in his poem *Nineteen Hundred and Nineteen* with the reference:

> *There lurches past, his great eyes without thought*
> *Under the shadow of stupid straw-pale locks,*
> *That insolent fiend Robert Artisson*
> *To whom the love-lorn Lady Kyteler brought*
> *Bronzed peacock feathers, red combs of her cocks.*

There have been at least four novels to date covering the events that led to Alice fleeing Ireland, offering different interpretations of her story and personality.[37] The idea has also been mooted that she was the inspiration behind Chaucer's *The Wife of Bath*.[38]

Then there is the strange tale of painter Paddy Shaw and author Claire Nolan, author of *The Stone*, a novel based on the events surrounding the Kyteler case. Five years before Nolan wrote her book, Shaw – inspired by the story of the infamous Kilkenny sorceress – painted a portrait of how he envisaged Alice. He kept the painting for some time, but could not shake the feeling that something was wrong. Several years later, he sent the image of Alice to Kyteler's Inn with the accompanying note: 'I painted this piece for myself. It didn't like living with me. I think she wanted to go home. So have her. Paddy Shaw.'

To further add to the mystery, the arrival of the painting caused quite a stir. According to some, Shaw's depiction of Alice bore a striking resemblance to Claire Nolan herself, who was as unaware of Paddy Shaw as he was of her when they finished their respective works on Alice.

Nearly 700 years on, the legend of Alice Kyteler continues to fascinate and inspire. Among the interpretations of her story there are also rumours that although she left Ireland in 1324, Alice did not abandon Kilkenny entirely. Visitors to Kyteler's Inn relate tales of strange sounds and disturbances, those who work there attributing the activity to the Inn's notorious former resident.

Whether a black-widow figure, the victim of a clash between State and Church or the victim of her own success, one thing is certain: Kilkenny is unlikely to ever forget Dame Alice Kyteler.

Chapter Two

Satan's Mistress: Agnes Waterhouse (1566)

There feminine dames attached were,
whom Satan had infect,
with Belials sprite whose sorcery did,
the simple so molest.

The Examination and Confession
of Certain Witches, 1566

The well-known image of the witch with her 'familiar' is a distinctly English concept.[1] Indeed, these companions are absent from all but a very few of the trials on the Continent for the period, and there is yet to be an entirely satisfactory explanation as to why this is so.[2]

A 'familiar' served several roles: providing information, granting wishes and terrorising those who had been rash enough to cross the suspected witch. The familiar was recognised as both proof and cause of the witch's malevolence, and while this spirit helper could take many forms they often appeared as animals, with dogs, mice and wild birds among others recorded in trial records throughout the period. Cats were a particularly popular form for a familiar to take, and the records are littered with references to the accused witch and her demonic cat that did her bidding.[3]

Agnes Waterhouse from Hatfield Peverel in Essex might have wished she had chosen her pet with more care. The elderly widow, along with her sister and her daughter Joan, was an early victim of the 1563 Act Against Conjurations, Enchantments, and Witchcrafts, which carried the death penalty for 'killing or destroying a person through witchcraft'. Fittingly, Agnes' tale begins with a cat by the name of Satan. She had been gifted the creature by her sister, Elizabeth Francis, who had in turn received it from her Grandmother, a local woman known as Mother Eve. Unlike the usual black cat associated with witches nowadays, Satan was white and by the time he reached Agnes must have been decidedly on the elderly side. Quite why her sister was passing him on is unclear – perhaps she felt Agnes had more need of his services than she did, or perhaps she was simply looking to rid herself of the need to care for an aged pet – but he would, Elizabeth assured Agnes, change her life. Her sister accordingly instructed Agnes in how to care for the cat; in return for some milk and the occasional sip of blood, Satan would grant whatever she asked for. Indeed, it later transpired that in the sixteen or so years that she had been his owner Elizabeth had made good use of the pet herself: availing herself of his powers to rid herself of two husbands, an unwanted child, and to have vengeance on those who vexed her in the village. What passed between the two women, and how much encouragement Agnes needed, goes unrecorded, but whatever occurred (and, if the two were sisters, it is worth wondering whether Agnes already had some inkling of what went on between her sister and the white cat, especially as she had been using the animal to get her way for more than a decade and a half) the animal was apparently exchanged for a cake and Agnes found herself with the dubious honour of becoming mistress to Satan.

Understandably, Agnes was keen to put her sister's claims to the test. The first thing she did was harmless enough: she 'willed' (the choice of wording in her confession) the cat to kill one of her own hogs. The experiment proved a success and the hog died. Mindful of what her sister had told her, Agnes gave the cat a chicken and a drop of blood obtained by pricking her own face or hand, and offering it to the cat to suck.

Either frightened by this success, or left feeling jubilant at her new-found power, it was not long before Agnes had cause again to put it to the test. After becoming aggrieved with a Father Kersye she sent the cat out to kill three of his hogs – whether in a flash of anger or coldly calculated is unclear, but the result was the same. The animals died, and Satan was again rewarded with a chicken and some blood. The cat was very thorough, as it was reported that even the bones and feathers of the bird had vanished by the time he had finished his meal, handily removing the evidence of his payment for the deed he had carried out at Agnes' behest.

After that, Agnes readily turned to Satan to redress the wrongs and injustices she felt had been dealt her by her neighbours. After a quarrel with Widow Goody she willed the cat to drown the other woman's cow and likewise, following an altercation with an unnamed woman, sent the cat to kill three of her geese. Further to this, when a neighbour refused to sell her yeast, she destroyed their brewing, and when denied butter by another, ruined this also. The most audacious of her attacks however, took place after a falling out with another neighbour and his wife; the couple so angered Agnes that she willed Satan to kill the man in question with a 'bloody flux'.[4]

The cat, when not carrying out Agnes' requests, was housed in a pot on a bed of wool. When, due to straitened circumstances, the old woman needed the wool, either to sell or to make use of elsewhere in the household, she discussed the matter with the cat at length before they reached the perfect solution. Agnes would turn Satan from a cat into a toad, which could then continue to live in the wool-less pot without any discomfort. This exchange duly took place, and Satan the cat became Satan the toad, with the relationship between mistress and familiar otherwise unchanged.

Matters came to a head in the summer of 1566. Agnes had left her 18-year-old daughter Joan at home one day as she went to Great Braxted, a village about five miles from Hatfield Peverel as the crow flies. Whilst her mother was absent, Joan visited the nearby Browne household where she asked 12-year-old Agnes Browne for some bread and cheese. Joan was greatly displeased when the child would not comply and decided to get her revenge. What transpired next frightened the girl terribly, and it was on her word that Elizabeth Francis, Agnes, and Joan were arrested on suspicion of witchcraft.

Agnes made a confession that was enough to condemn her outright, and, because she pleaded guilty, did not need to stand trial.[5] She was present at Joan's trial however, and it was there that the whole story unfolded.

Questioned in court, Joan Waterhouse told how her mother had wished her to learn witchcraft and tried to persuade her to do so on many occasions. She had always refused, knowing that it was the wrong thing to do, but what she had witnessed gave her an idea for how to get her revenge on Agnes Browne. Greatly vexed by the altercation with the girl, Joan admitted she had returned home and, as she had heard her mother do, called for Satan to come and do her bidding. The animal had appeared, not as a cat or a toad, but in the guise of a black dog from under her mother's bed. When asked what she wanted, Joan admitted she had told it to go to young Agnes and scare her. She offered a red cock in payment (somewhat belying her insistence that she knew nothing of what her mother did or how to do it) but the dog refused, saying that instead he would have her body and soul. The young woman, understandably terrified by this, agreed in order to make the creature go away. Much to her relief, the dog left her, going on his way to torment young Agnes.

Agnes Browne told the court that a large black dog had appeared while she was churning butter and scared her half to death. The dog was no ordinary dog and had, said the girl, the face of an ape, with a silver whistle on a chain about its neck. Not only that, the creature had horns on its head and carried in its mouth the key to the door of the milk house. When Agnes asked what he wanted, the dog declared that he would have some butter; he would not take no for an answer and, after some argument, the intruder ran to the milk-house door, unlocked it and went inside. After spending some time inside, he emerged to declare that he had made 'flap' butter.[6] Much to the girl's relief the dog then left and she quickly ran to tell her aunt. The local priest was called in turn, and when the clergyman arrived he told Agnes Browne to pray and call on the name of Jesus. This was timely advice as the following day the dog appeared again, holding the key to the milk house in his mouth as before. When Agnes asked what in the name of Jesus he was holding, the creature grew agitated, telling her that she was speaking wicked words before leaving. Unfortunately, this was far from the end of the matter, and the strange dog continued to appear to Agnes, who each time would speak in the name of Jesus to cause the creature to depart again.

There came a period when she was not troubled by such visitations and it was hoped that the dog had tired of his game. The relief was short-lived though as the next time Agnes Browne saw the dog he came holding a knife, with which he threatened to kill her. When Agnes begged him to set down the knife and spare her life, the creature refused, cryptically declaring that he would not leave his 'sweet dame's' knife. Although deeply frightened, the girl managed to ask for the name of his mistress and, in reply, he gestured with his head towards the home of Agnes Waterhouse.

When Agnes Waterhouse was asked by the Queen's Attorney for a response, Agnes asked the girl what type of knife had been used in the threat. Agnes Browne replied that it was a dagger.

'Marry my lord,' Agnes responded triumphantly, 'She saith it is a dagger knife, and I have none such in my house, but a great knife, and therein she lieth.'[7]

Joan Waterhouse agreed that the girl must be lying because her mother was right regarding the lack of a dagger in the household. She also questioned the mention of the creature having a face like an ape, for it had been most definitely a dog, and only a dog, when she had sent it on its way to do her bidding.

What the Queen's attorney made of that can only be guessed at, but he proceeded to make Agnes an offer. If Agnes could make the dog appear before them in the courtroom, he personally would make sure that she was freed from prison. Agnes was not in a position to accept this potential reprieve however, lamenting that she could not do so. As she explained, Joan had taken control of the creature and now she, Agnes, had no power over it, unable to call it off or make it do anything as she had not been the one to send it out.[8]

Agnes was then asked when Satan had last had blood from her. Despite already having confessed, Agnes now denied that she had ever let the familiar do such a thing. The matter was pushed however and the scarf Agnes was wearing was lifted to reveal several spots on her face and one on her nose – incriminating enough for the attorney to repeat his question. Caving, Agnes responded: 'Not this fortnight'; a damning declaration indeed as the jury retired to consider the evidence against Joan.[9]

The outcome was mixed for the women of Hatfield Peverel. Despite her tormenting of Agnes Browne, Joan Waterhouse was found innocent. Elizabeth Francis was declared guilty, sentenced to a term of imprisonment but Agnes was not to be as fortunate.[10] She had confessed to the murder by witchcraft of William Fynee, a fellow resident of Hatfield Peverel, and was condemned to death under the terms of the recently passed Act.[11]

On 29 July 1566, Agnes went to the gallows, earning the dubious honour of being the first woman in England to be executed for witchcraft.

Readers of the pamphlet account of the case are assured that the old woman confessed 'most earnestly' to being a witch and that she had carried out witchcraft against many for the last 15 years.[12] She also, like a good Christian, repented everything she had done and begged forgiveness from God for her many crimes.

If the record is to be taken as accurate, the crowd of onlookers demanded answers from the condemned witch. The first question was whether Agnes had sent Satan to a man named Wardol, a tailor with whom she had cause to be at odds, with the intention of bringing harm to himself and his belongings. Agnes said that she had indeed sent Satan on such an errand, but that she had found herself unable to do anything to harm him as the man's faith was so strong that her power was useless.

The onlookers also wanted to know whether Agnes was a regular churchgoer. Agnes replied in the affirmative, and when questioned as to what exactly she did when in church, she assured her listeners that she prayed as any good Christian would do. Indeed, she said *The Lord's Prayer*, *Ave Maria* and *The Belief*, or *Creed*, though not in English as was now the official tongue of the Elizabethan Church. When pressed by those gathered, Agnes admitted that she said them in Latin, as Satan would not allow her to do otherwise.

The account ends by informing the reader that:

> *for these and many other offences which she had committed, done and confessed she bewailed, repented, and asked mercy of God, and all the world forgiveness, and thus she yielded up her soul, trusting to be in joy with Christ her saviour, which dearly had bought her with his most precious blood.*[13]

It is not possible to know the mood of the crowd that day. Curiosity, no doubt, played a part; one might also think pity at an old woman's plight, or relief and gladness to see the end of the woman whom they suspected had been the cause of much of their misery over the last decade and a half. It is not recorded whether Joan Waterhouse, about to be made an orphan by the noose, attended the execution; nor Elizabeth Francis, the sister that no doubt thanked her lucky stars that she had, for now at least, escaped the same fate.[14]

The Parish Registers for Hatfield Peverel are only available from the seventeenth century, the earliest over half a century too late to be of any help piecing together Agnes' family. Therefore, there is no way of knowing what Agnes' maiden name was and if any of her former family remained to either know or care when she was accused and condemned. Indeed, little is known of her family or background other than that she had a daughter, Joan, and that her older sister Elizabeth had taken the surname of her husband John Francis.[15]

What became of 'Satan' after the death of his mistress is unknown. While pets tended to have 'pet' or human names, the naming of Agnes' cat stands out as being particularly blatant for its diabolical connection, and is likely to have caused considerable suspicion.[16]

It has been argued that 'the cat's association with magic, heresy and witchcraft relates in part to its peculiar status as being both domesticated and wild,' something that proved difficult to reconcile.[17] Despite this, it did not become illegal to consort with a familiar until 1604 when the act passed in that year stated that 'if any person or persons … shall use, practise, or exercise any invocation or conjuration of any evil and wicked spirit; or shall consult, covenant with, entertain, employ, feed, or reward any evil and wicked spirit to or for any intent or purpose' they were to suffer death.[18] Agnes, therefore, was not guilty on that particular count of an offence punishable by death despite the accusations – and her own admission of consorting with Satan in his several forms.

The concept of a familiar sucking blood from a witch had several potential meanings and became a well-known feature of witchcraft cases. One suggestion is that it marked the physical sign of the pact between the witch and her familiar.[19] There has also been a general misunderstanding and conflation of the idea of giving a spot of blood for reward and the actual sucking of blood from the witch's body.[20] The latter was not something that was part of Agnes' story, and it is clear from the tale that only a small amount of blood was taken. The spots where Satan had taken blood were, it was made clear, still showing on Agnes' face for all to see when she was questioned in court.

In Agnes' case, the familiar also had prophetic properties, as Agnes had stated that she had been warned of her arrest and future suffering by Satan.[21] The very concept of keeping animals as pets was viewed as somewhat morally suspect, and the stigma of the cat is something that has not entirely changed – the stereotype of the old woman with her cats is very much alive today.

There is little doubt that those involved in the trial of Agnes believed in the Devil: witchcraft, familiars and demon dogs were very real features of life. When Agnes Browne related her tale of the demon dog threatening her with the knife, neither Agnes or her daughter Joan (nor indeed anyone else in attendance) debated the possibility of the existence of such a creature – their objection was only that the type of knife described by the girl did not match one that Agnes possessed and therefore the witness must have been fabricating or embroidering her story.[22]

Another point of note in Agnes' confession was her admitting that 'because she lived somewhat unquietly with her husband she caused Satan to kill him, and he did so about nine years past, since which time she had lived as a widow.'[23] Her sister, Elizabeth, also confessed to killing her own husband after living in discord with him, perhaps setting a precedent that Agnes decided to follow.

Why or when Agnes and her husband married is not recorded. In the period in question, matches were made for a variety of reasons, ranging from the emotional to the purely practical and economic. However well they got on with their husbands, women were expected to accept their inferior status and remain quietly subordinate to their spouses. Whether rich or poor, these ideas were perpetuated through every channel of society, preached from the pulpit, marital handbooks, popular culture and that of the classes above filtering down. Wives were encouraged on all levels to be docile and amenable.[24]

By her own admission, Agnes did not fit this stereotype of wifely submissiveness. Whether this lack of harmony within the marriage was restricted to a purely verbal form or whether it strayed over into the physical is not clear. During the time in question, it was not illegal for husbands to beat their wives – in fact they were given free rein to use 'moderate correction' upon their spouses as they saw fit.[25] This, however, could lead to wildly varying interpretations, and was open to much abuse. Excessive violence towards wives was experienced among all levels of society; indeed a sixteenth century London by-law forbade the beating of wives after 9 pm due to the noise disturbing neighbours.[26]

When faced with an abusive or unhappy marriage, a woman's options for escape were few. Once married, she had no property of her own and very little in the way of rights. She could run away, but it would be difficult to support herself. If a wife had been engaged in an affair, there was the chance of a 'wife-sale', but the outcome might not leave her in any better a position

than if she had left of her own accord. Legal separation was also an option –
'a mensa et thoro' (separation from bed and board) meant that a wife could
live apart from her husband, but did not allow either to remarry. It also came
at a cost, which Agnes might not have been able to afford.[27]

Suicide was another decidedly drastic option, and not one resorted to
with great frequency. There was great stigma attached for one thing, both to
the suicide and the family left behind. It also put the immortal soul in grave
danger, a result that only the extremely desperate would risk.

There was another resort available to wives who wanted to be rid of their
husbands: murder. It was this option that Agnes admitted to having chosen,
using her inherited familiar to do the dreadful deed. Despite her admission
of guilt however this was not an indictment that Agnes was charged on and
it is highly likely that she had no further involvement in his death than the
unfortunate fact of having wished it.[28]

Whatever her role in her husband's death however, Agnes was left a
widow, and whatever her economic status beforehand, this would likely have
plunged her deeper into poverty. Those who had a good reputation and
whose situation had been unavoidable could often receive poor relief from
the authorities or charity from neighbours. This was very much on a moral
basis however, and if there was a hint of any misconduct, then help would be
withdrawn.[29] The authorities were also aiming to force the poor to fend for
themselves, and older children were charged with supporting their elderly
parents.[30]

Agnes' position was not uncommon; evidence shows that there were twice
as many widows as widowers in the population as a whole, partly due to the
fact that women were often younger than their husbands and therefore had
a greater likelihood of being left when their spouse died.[31]

Although the case took place during the reign of the Protestant Elizabeth
I, Agnes, born around the turn of the century if the age given in the record
of her case is accurate, had lived through the greatest upheaval the English
church had witnessed; the Reformation. For her to be saying her prayers
in Latin, therefore, whether directed to by Satan or not, would not be so
remarkable or subversive as it was simply the language in which she had
learned them. However, Elizabethan legislation decreed that all prayers
and sermons had to be conducted in English and there were penalties for

those who didn't comply. Latin was a staple of the Catholic Church, and Catholic prayers were, in fact, seen as little better than magic and witchcraft themselves, with priests accused of being magicians in league with the Devil. Agnes' admission that she said everything in Latin because Satan would not allow her to do otherwise only served to confirm what was already suspected: Agnes was working with the Devil and was now paying the price.

Agnes is commemorated in Judy Chicago's art installation *The Dinner Party*, along with several other women who lost their lives due to accusations of witchcraft.[32] Although not one of England's most 'popular' witches, her case, without doubt, shaped and influenced the future of English witchcraft trials.

Chapter Three

Charms and Witches: Gwen ferch Ellis (1594)

In the name of God the father, the son, and the holy spirit of God,
And the three Marys, and the three consecrated altars,
And the blessed son of grace,
And by the stones, and by the herbs,
To which the son of grace bestowed their virtues
In order that they should defend thee, the sinner who suffered adversity,
As Christ [Himself] defended [you.]

Charm recited by Gwen ferch Ellis – 1594[1]

Erroneously considered one of Britain's more backward and less civilised outposts for a large part of history, Wales still, on occasion bears the brunt of such prejudices even today. There were advantages to this perception however, as it meant that Wales, unlike the South of England, was shielded from the increase in witchcraft persecutions seen in the latter in the second half of the sixteenth century.[2] That's not to say that the Welsh did not believe in witches, quite the opposite; it is clear that the concept of witchcraft was ingrained within popular culture. But the response was very different due to the pre-existence of Welsh Customary Law and, for that reason, Wales never saw the same wash of witchcraft trials and executions that took place in England.[3]

Gwen ferch Ellis, a woman from Betws-yn-Rhos in Conwy, North Wales, was to prove an exception to this rule. Gwen lived with her third husband, John ap Morrice and made her living in the same manner as many women in the area: spinning and weaving to produce cloth to sell at market. She also had another role in the community: providing medicine to cure sick animals. Her plasters and salves were much sought after and Gwen developed a reputation, not only for helping animals but also using words and potions to help men, women and children who were sick or in need of the services she could offer. This trade was both lucrative – the payments she received in kind providing most of her support – and also her downfall.

The situation created by the Reformation was somewhat bleak to say the least; the comfort and protection that had been given by the old church was removed, and at the same time great stress was placed upon the existence and power of the Devil.[4] People were therefore left feeling under threat but with little in the way of reassurance or practical ways in which they could defend and protect themselves. Gwen's charms were, as it can be imagined, in great demand.

All might have continued on as it was but, in May or early June of 1594, a written charm was discovered at Gloddaith, the house of the influential Mostyn family. The charm caused great consternation not only because it had been hidden in the parlour there, but due to the fact that it was written backwards; a sure sign (it was believed) that harm had been intended towards Thomas Mostyn and his family. Due to her reputation, Gwen's name was mentioned in connection with the discovery, though it is unclear who first pointed the finger. Her friends advised her to leave the area, but Gwen refused to run when she could confidently say that she had nothing to do with the matter. She would have done well to heed the warnings as she was arrested a short while later by William Hughes, Bishop of St Asaph and taken to Flint Castle.

After being questioned regarding her life and how she made a living, the interrogation turned to the delicate matter of witchcraft and charming. Gwen admitted that she had used her knowledge of charming to help those in need, readily recounting examples of when she had done so. Her sister Elizabeth, long dead, had taught her how to charm and it was clear that Gwen saw no harm in it. Gwen's house had been searched, no doubt for evidence that would corroborate her involvement with the charm at Gloddaith, and, although there was nothing concrete, there were two discoveries that made things look rather bad for Gwen – a bell without its clapper and a figure of Christ showing him rising from the dead. These objects had come from her sister, but she had not used them for charming or any other purpose. Nevertheless, the connections that could be made to the ways of the 'old' Catholic Church were enough to raise suspicions.

It seems that it was not only her charming work but also her association with a member of another powerful local family, the Conways, that led to suspicions being voiced about Gwen. There had been a dispute between the Conway family and the Mostyns; and Jane Conway, widow and matriarch of Marle Hall in Conwy, was a known associate of Gwen's.

When questioned, Gwen conceded that she had received from Jane Conway two copies of St John's Gospel, (these were apparently written out by Jane's son, Hugh Holland) and a charm of a similar nature was discovered in Gwen's bag. She also, intriguingly, admitted to having stayed at Gloddaith for a night once about two years before the charm was found; the reason was not given, but Thomas Mostyn was away, which was seen as decidedly suspicious. One thing was very clear however: Gwen categorically denied leaving the charm at Gloddaith.

Whilst in prison, Gwen was questioned further on the matter of Jane Conway, the implication being that Jane Conway had engaged Gwen to get her own back on Thomas Mostyn with whom she had quarrelled. Gwen was firm that she had not left the charm at Gloddaith, but mentioned that she *had* seen something of that nature: in Jane Conway's prayer book. When asked about the charm discovered at Thomas Mostyn's house, Jane's son Hugh Holland said he had not written it, although he had written out John's Gospel and given it to his mother, thus confirming Gwen's assertions and creating a potentially dangerous situation for Jane Conway and her family.

Although Gwen told her questioners how she had been assured that Jane would not see her left without help, she admitted that matters were not so clear now. She had recently been visited in prison by two women who had warned her that Jane Conway was unhappy; Gwen should not have spoken of what she and Gwen had discussed regarding Thomas Mostyn nor the matter of the charms.[5]

Despite Gwen's protestations of innocence, on 12 July local magistrates were given the power to gather witnesses against her. On 30 August, those who had evidence to give were gathered at the parish church of Dyserth, and told what they knew. How long the witnesses had waited for a chance to speak out against Gwen before this opportunity is unclear; the earliest incident recorded was from six years previously but there could have been rumblings against her long before that. Whatever the case, the stories related before the two justices were damning indeed.

A tale from 1591 that had rankled enough to be remembered concerned William Griffith ap William, the bailiff of Is Dulas. Spurred on by others perhaps, he decided to put Gwen's reputed powers to the test. Accordingly, he had informed Gwen that she should expect a visit from himself and some associates, with the added twist that he would not reveal the time or date, asserting that, given Gwen's supposed abilities, she should have no trouble in being able to predict when they would be coming and prepare to receive them. As promised, the bailiff and his party arrived unannounced one evening, telling Gwen that they wanted drink. They were willing to pay for whatever Gwen provided, but, resenting the intrusion and inconvenience, she refused. Although they were already in the house by that point she decided to make a stand, her back to the cellar door to reinforce her point that none would be drinking what lay beyond.

Robert Evans, one of William Griffith's party, took matters a step too far and laid hands upon Gwen, pushing her aside. At this display of force and no doubt realising she was outnumbered, Gwen capitulated, but not before making it clear that revenge would be sought against any who had done her harm. Thus venting her anger, she sent her maid to fetch drink for the assembled intruders. Once they were finished, Gwen herself went for more. She returned with a large jug containing the desired liquid, but the men were perturbed to see a large fly floating in it. Try as they might, they could not remove the intruding insect, its size and strange behaviour leaving the assembled drinkers with the strong suspicion that they were actually confronting Gwen's familiar demon. Finally, the jug was knocked onto the floor, but the bailiff's expected triumph at getting the better of the creature soured when the fly was nowhere to be seen. Gwen's vow of revenge was not forgotten and it was said that she got her own back within the fortnight. Robert Evans, who had so rashly manhandled Gwen, found himself with a broken arm – and, as coincidence would have it, the very same arm that he had used to push Gwen. To add to the matter the bailiff's own wife was taken ill, languishing miserably and suffering the loss of use of her arms and legs.

Griffith ap Hugh, from Betws, also had something to say about Gwen. His mother had consulted her in the summer of 1592 regarding an ox that had been lost. Gwen was offered a 'hoop' of rye in payment if she could reveal the whereabouts of the missing animal and replied with confidence that it would be found in Gwytherin.[6] Unfortunately for Gwen, the ox finally turned up several miles away from the place she had named and, consequently, she was denied the agreed payment. Gwen was unimpressed with this outcome and made her unhappiness clear, though her complaint did not alter the outcome: she was left grumbling and empty handed. The following year, Griffith's brother David fell ill. Gwen was asked to visit to see the stricken man and no sign of animosity during the visit was recorded. She brought with her a drink for the sick man and, in addition, used a charm made of salt to help speed his recovery. Unfortunately, David's condition worsened instead of getting better. Not only that, but he was convinced that, although the medicinal drink had done him no harm, the charm with the salt was another matter, asserting that it would be the cause of his death.

The most damning evidence, however, came from Elin ferch Richard, a 60-year old widow from Llaneilian-yn-Rhos, where Gwen had lived with her second husband. Her tale went back to 1589, when her husband had employed Gwen's second husband at his mill. Trouble had come when Elin's son, Lewis ap John, had argued with Gwen. The cause of the dispute is, as is often the case, unrecorded, but the result was that the young man hit Gwen. Not long afterwards, Lewis ap John fell into a strange madness and neighbours declared that Gwen had taken her revenge on him. The young man died on the very day, according to his mother, that Gwen said he would.

Based on the evidence taken by the witnesses, there were three indictments drawn up against Gwen. That she had broken Robert Evans' arm through witchcraft; that she had bewitched the bailiff's wife, Lowri ferch John ap Ieuan, causing her to lose the use of her arms and legs; and, finally and most fatally for Gwen, that she had been responsible for the death of Lewis ap John, son of Elin ferch Richard, by witchcraft.[7]

There are no written records of what took place in the courtroom during Gwen's trial in October of 1594, but the verdict was unequivocal – Gwen was found guilty and sentenced to death by hanging.[8]

Gwen's execution marked the first in Wales for witchcraft. Her appearance in court was remarkable enough in itself. It was uncommon for a woman to reach trial on a matter of life and death in the Welsh courts of the time for any reason at all, and women were an uncommon sight at the sessions in general, making up less than ten per cent of prisoners at most court sessions.[9] It was even more of an anomaly for the death sentence to be actually carried out; of the thirty-seven suspects featuring in thirty-two witchcraft cases in Wales between 1568 and 1698, only eight verdicts of guilty were returned, and of those eight, only five suffered the full penalty for their supposed crimes.[10] The reference to Gwen's fly 'familiar' also sets her case apart. Although a feature of English witchcraft cases from the middle of the sixteenth century, familiars did not generally play a role in Welsh witchcraft accusations.[11] It should also be noted that a fly was a somewhat unusual choice for a demon in any case; the most common examples were cats, dogs, toads and mice, with flies featuring only a handful of times in the testimonies given in English cases.[12] Gwen's familiar also stands out as it did not have a name; most familiars were named in the records that mention them.[13] Linked to this is the fact that the Devil tends not to feature in Welsh cases so Gwen's fly familiar being referenced as the 'devil's minion' in the testimony against her is somewhat remarkable.[14] There is only one other case of the time where the Devil is referred to, and that is the case of Margaret ferch Richard who was apparently seduced by the Devil although it is not entirely clear what is meant by the term 'devil' in this instance.

Gwen was also not the 'stereotypical witch' seen elsewhere. Far from being elderly and destitute, she was only around forty years of age at the time of her arrest and would have been younger still at the time of the first incidents cited against her. She was also wealthy enough to employ a maid and so not of the poorest section of society. That she had wealth and a certain degree of economic independence can also be inferred from references to her work both as a weaver and for her services as a charmer, for which she was often paid in kind, receiving the commodities she needed, such as butter, in exchange for her work.[15]

Another area where Gwen's case stands out is that of the seven witnesses who spoke out against her, five were men; a distinct contrast from England where women were most likely to speak out against those suspected of witchcraft. This reflects the community-based nature of witchcraft accusations, and the suspicions that grew up over time, along with the difference in nature between the English and Welsh cases.

From the information given by Gwen herself it seems that she was about twenty years of age when she first married. This marriage, to Lewis ap David ap Gwyn, lasted only two years before her husband died, though the cause of death is not given. She was luckier second time around and her marriage to Lewis ap David ap Griffith Gethin lasted eighteen years before he too died. She had also lived in various places: moving from Llandyrnog to her uncle's home in Yale thence to Llaneilian-yn-Rhos, where her second husband owned a mill, before finally settling in Betws-yn-Rhos. Born in Llandyrnog in the Vale of Clwyd, she had lived with her uncle from the age of about five, with nothing known of her parents or other family members. Whether she had children is uncertain, but there is no mention of any in the records of her case. There is also no further reference to Gwen's husband John ap Morrice, meaning that we have no idea of how he responded to the accusations against his wife, nor how he was treated by his neighbours or whether he thought her guilty or innocent.

Gwen was well known for the help she provided both in her community and farther afield, and was obviously a popular choice when people needed aid. People came from great distances to visit her; she refers for instance to a child from Caerhun, Caernarfonshire whom she had helped with her charms.[16] She also clearly had a reputation strong enough to be put to the test by the bailiff in 1591.

Such renown could often be a double-edged sword, and along with this reputation for being able to help, Gwen was attributed with a trait that was common in witchcraft accusations: a vengeful personality. In the evidence and complaints against Gwen, much is made of this and the behaviour that resulted; this less-than-desirable trait was used as both explanation for, and proof of, the actions that caused so much suffering. After all, why else would she wish someone ill, unless she was vengeful at heart, and why else would someone fall ill after a run-in with Gwen unless she had willed it to happen?[17]

The role of a charmer or 'cunning person' in Welsh society was somewhat problematic and difficult to balance, both for those who held it and those who sought their services. On the one hand, cunning folk were reputed to be able to help those in need and were often called in cases where more conventional methods had failed to provide relief. On the other, if a condition did not improve or, more disastrously, deteriorated, then the cunning man or woman found themselves in danger of censure and perhaps worse. This delicate balance and dual belief is clear in the case of Elin ferch Richard's son, Lewis ap John; the mother went to ask Gwen to set her son right, seeing her as not only the cause of his suffering, but also her only remaining hope for a cure. The two opinions, of her profession and personality, were able to co-exist, with either one at the fore at any given moment. It was the tipping of the scales towards focus on her more vengeful elements that brought disaster to Gwen.

Although the legislation of the 1542 and 1563 Witchcraft Acts appears to have been targeted at cunning folk more than at witches, in practice there is no evidence to show that the ruling English took enough notice of Welsh cunning folk and charmers to launch an attack against them in any noticeable numbers.[18] There is also nothing to show that they were in more danger of being charged at the end of the century, when Gwen's case took place, than they had been at the start; again highlighting a difference between English and Welsh cases.[19]

Gwen didn't seem reluctant to share information on how she had come to charm or how she performed her work, and the overriding impression throughout is that she considered herself to be doing nothing wrong. That she believed she had power to heal the people and animals put into her care is not in question; Gwen openly said that people believed she could heal them and therefore she believed that she could do the things said of her.[20] This belief was not uncommon and ran the danger of becoming a self-fulfilling prophecy, one that could spiral out of control and lead to the accused believing that she had done the terrible things either testified against her in court or whispered by her neighbours. Gwen, however, does not seem to have gone that far; believing in her powers, but not in her guilt, and remaining steadfast to the end that she had not set the charm against Thomas Mostyn. It is interesting to note that, apart from Gwen, the women in Welsh cases admitted their guilt and took responsibility for causing the harm of which they were accused. The fact that Gwen did not makes her case stand out because her denial of responsibility made the usual pattern of admission and repentance, which often led to the accused walking away, impossible.[21]

Labels are important, however, and the first use of the word 'witch' against Gwen can be dated to the incident in 1591 when the bailiff and his party imposed on her at home. The bailiff's wife, in her suffering, had no doubts as to Gwen's ability, and summoned her to their house to make her well. Gwen's response had been that she could help if the other woman believed in her. This no doubt gave the ailing woman hope, but the bailiff was not so pleased to come home to find Gwen tending to his wife. Not only that, he discovered the woman he considered responsible for his wife's illness standing over the cradle of their child – this was beyond the limits of acceptability and his displeasure was deeply apparent. Things were smoothed over enough so that Gwen could leave without a scene, but in the aftermath he demanded of his wife why Gwen, that 'witch' had been in his house. This was the first time that the term was used against Gwen that we know of, marking the definite shift from white and 'good magic' to black and 'destructive magic'.[22]

Another area where there was a blurring of lines between religion and the work of cunning folk with their charms was apparent in the Reformation. The ways of the old Catholic church were seen by the Protestant reformers as magic and superstition, and any hint of these continuing to exist was taken as a remnant of 'simpler times' which needed to be stamped out in much the same way as modern thinkers tend to disregard people in the past as 'simple' and credulous in their belief in magic and religion. To further confuse matters, the priests of the 'old' religion were actively involved in practices that were considered to be synonymous with magic.[23] In 1589, people of North Wales still crossed themselves when they shut their windows, when they left their cattle, and when they left houses in the morning. If something bad befell them or their animals, the common saying was 'you have not crossed yourself well today' or 'you have not made the sign of the rood upon the cattle' and the belief was that omission had caused mishap, further illustrating the magic of the medieval church.[24] There was also a belief that the churching practice, that of making a woman clean again and ready to participate in the life of the church after she had given birth, was a charm against witchcraft. This remained the case as late as the end of the seventeenth century.[25] Although she denied their use in her charming, the clapperless bell and the image of Christ found at Gwen's house, and the suspicion these created also highlights the connection between the old religion and witchcraft, both in real terms and in the eyes of the authorities.

Bells were certainly believed to have great power, being rung during storms and also to scare away disease and plague.[26]

Written charms, of the sort that sparked the trial against Gwen, could vary in complexity from just a few simple lines to the longer and more involved and were usually religious in nature.[27] The religious connection to charming is illustrated clearly in the charm that was in Gwen's bag when questioned by the bishop:

In the name of God the father, the son, and the holy spirit of God,
And the three Marys, and the three consecrated altars,
And the blessed son of grace,
And by [literally on] the stones, and by [on] the herbs,
To which the son of grace [Jesus] bestowed their virtues
In order that they should defend thee, the sinner who suffered adversity,
As Christ [himself] defended [you.]

In the name of the Father, the Son, and the Holy Spirit,
Against adversity above wind, against adversity below wind,
Against adversity above ground and below ground,
Against adversity of [the] middle of the world,
And against adversity in [any] place in the world,
God keep you and preserve you from a wolf of a man,
From the evil thing of hell [Satan].
I take thee to be a child of God,
And a follower of Christ and an heir
to the kingdom of heaven.[28]

Many charms were little more than sections of the gospels copied out and the Gospel of John was particularly prevalent due to a belief that it held protective powers, especially after the Reformation, and this belief continued well into the seventeenth century in Wales.[29] It is interesting that the charms Gwen said she had seen in Jane Conway's possession were copies of John's Gospel. Were Jane and her son involved in creating charms themselves, or had her son merely written out the Gospel for their own protection? In light of the feud with Mostyn, this could be particularly instructive. It was common for a charm to be concealed, if not worn on the person; popular places were above doors or windows.[30] This was the case with the charm found at Gloddaith and one wonders whether the charm was *intended* to be found, making it a potential warning.

Although things did not look good for Gwen given the evidence cited against her, the outcome of her trial was not a forgone conclusion. There is evidence that the final indictment against Gwen caused some controversy among the jury considering her case. The first two, the laming and injuring of her supposed victims, were punishable by imprisonment for a year and a turn in the pillory under the 1563 Witchcraft Act. Causing death by witchcraft, on the other hand, turned simple maleficium into murder, a felony for which the punishment was death. There is evidence on the documents themselves that it was not an easy decision to make – although the words 'billa vera' or 'true bill', meaning that the jury agreed with the judgement, are clear on the indictment document. 'Ignoramus' is also present, fainter, but proving that initially the jury decided that they did not find the final indictment to hold.[31]

What led to the harsher verdict? The case hinged around the involvement of the prominent families of Mostyn and Conway. It seems that Jane Conway had called upon Gwen around Christmas time 1592, telling her of her issues with Thomas Mostyn. The troubles appear to have been financial, though no further details are available. Jane asked Gwen for information regarding Mostyn and his finances, asking where he kept his money and for how long the man would live. There was also a tale regarding Mostyn sending his money away for safe keeping, only for the horse taking it to meet with an accident. Gwen related how she had told Jane that she knew nothing, either of Thomas Mostyn's financial affairs or of what had befallen the animal taking his money away.[32]

Through her actions and rash words, Jane Conway had put herself and the reputation of her family in a precarious position. Jane, as the widow of Hugh Holland of Conwy, would have known better than anyone the dangers of dabbling in witchcraft.[33] Out of her eleven surviving children, two of her sons were to publish anti-witchcraft texts during the closing years of the sixteenth century; both Robert and Henry Holland published works against witchcraft and, although for different audiences and in different tones, their essential meanings were the same. These works provide a useful insight into how witchcraft was viewed in Wales at the time. The appearance of the two unnamed women to see Gwen in prison is also suspicious and points to Jane Conway being more involved in the case of the Mostyn charm than she might like to admit. Although people in Wales would be familiar with what was going on in England through the witchcraft pamphlets that had been increasing in popularity from the mid–sixteenth century, Jane had little reason to worry unless she had indeed been involved in someway. That she was worried Gwen had spoken out of turn is clear.

Thomas Mostyn may also have had his reasons for wanting to see Gwen prosecuted and removed. The eldest son of William Mostyn, Thomas inherited from his father upon his death in 1576 and was, eventually, the first member of the family to be knighted. He was twice sheriff of Anglesey and Flintshire, and also sheriff of Caernarvonshire as well as Justice of the Peace for the same three areas; positions he retained until his death in 1618.[34] The prominence of the family is obvious when Sir William Russell, appointed Lord Deputy for Ireland in 1594, stayed at Gloddaith on 21 July 1594, not long after Gwen's imprisonment.[35]

The Mostyn family had real authority within the community; if they thought Gwen was responsible for a potentially dangerous charm or warning that might bring misfortune, they had the power to push for her punishment. What took place was also a powerful and prominent message to the Conway family, warning Jane Conway in particular not to think they could act against the Mostyns and get away with it.[36] Tellingly, there were more connections between those involved with Gwen's case than first meets the eye. William Hughes, the Bishop of Asaph, who first arrested Gwen, was closely connected to Thomas Mostyn – his daughter married Mostyn two years after Gwen's trial and execution. Hughes had been chaplain to the fourth Duke of Norfolk around 1560, and died in 1600.[37]

There is also speculation over whether Gwen was ever actually executed at all. Despite the guilty verdict, there is no record of her execution or her death, and it would be nice to think that she did, at the last, escape the fate that was decreed for her. Survival was the normal outcome for Welsh witch trials even when guilt was established; a guilty verdict did not automatically lead to execution even when the law dictated it.[38] However, it is clear from the documents relating to Gwen's case that she *was* found guilty and the death penalty decided; as there is no record of this being overturned or a pardon granted, then it is logical, albeit sadly so, to conclude that she did go to the noose. It is also unwise to talk of Gwen's case too much in the context of Welsh trials as her case was vitally different in the fact that it involved two of the influential families in the locality. She was caught up in something much bigger than herself and her case does not fit the standard pattern of Welsh cases for the period.[39] In this case, Gwen was arrested in relation to the finding of the charm at Gloddaith, and it was the evidence given by those brought in to be questioned that gave the excuse to remove her. This is in direct contrast to the more usual cases of malefice where the desired end result was restoring the status quo within the community and to have the parties involved reconciled to each other.

If Gwen did go free, then she vanished from the historical record as abruptly as she entered it, the only proof of her existence being the documents relating to her arrest and questioning. In fact, if she had not been arrested it is unlikely we would know anything of her at all, leaving her existence to pass, forgotten and unknown, into the mists of time.

Chapter Four

To Swim a Witch: Mary Sutton (1612)

The other is their fleeting on the water: for as in a secret murder, if the dead carcase be at any time thereafter handled by the murderer, it will gush out of blood, as if the blood were crying to the heaven for revenge of the murderer God having appointed that secret supernatural sign, for trial of that secrete unnatural crime, so it appears that God has appointed (for a supernatural sign of the monstrous impiety of the Witches) that the water shall refuse to receive them in her bosom, that have shaken off them the sacred Water of Baptism, and wilfully refused the benefit thereof.

Daemonologie, James I, 1597

There were many ways to detect a witch: asking the suspect to recite the Lord's Prayer; weighing her against the Church bible and searching for marks on her body that betrayed her allegiance to the Devil. The one that has stuck most in the popular imagination, however, is the swimming test. The suspected witch was lowered into a body of water; if she sank, she was innocent, embraced by the water (and probably somewhat the worse for it), and if guilty she would float, rejected by the water of baptism for all to see.

Mary Sutton would discover this to her cost. Living with her widowed mother in Milton Ernest, a village three miles from Bedford, she helped the elderly Mother Sutton as any good daughter would do. However, there was rumoured to be a more sinister reason for her apparent devotion; Mother Sutton was a witch, and Mary was well-versed in her mother's dark arts.

It had not always been so; initially the Suttons had been well-regarded, with Mother Sutton given the job of tending the local hogs to help ease her poverty. Things had carried on well for the space of about twenty years, with the Sutton women seen in a nothing but positive light. True, there were several incidents where animals had died unexpectedly, or some other mishap had occurred, but no one started to suspect that Mary and her mother might be responsible until a particular incident opened the eyes of the people of Milton Ernest.[1]

As is often the case, a disagreement over something too trivial even to be recorded was the catalyst that brought this happy arrangement to an end. Mother Sutton quarrelled with a local gentleman named Master Inger, and it was said that in her ire she decided to take revenge.[2]

Inger's horses were afflicted first – although they had been well when left at night, come morning they were dead: either strangled or beaten to death. Worse, with some the cause of death could not even be guessed at and the poor beasts were simply found dead in their stalls. That was not the end of it; Inger's swine also started to behave in a peculiar fashion, tearing out their own innards and attacking their fellow animals. Groups of between ten and twenty would suddenly take leave of their senses, running into the mill dam where they drowned themselves before anyone could stop them. In the space of two years he had, he was sure, lost money to the tune of two hundred pounds due to what he now considered to be the machinations of Mother Sutton.

During the same period Henry Sutton, the illegitimate son of Mary Sutton, had a run in with an old servant of Master Inger's.[3] The boy was throwing mud and stones into the mill dam and when asked to stop by the man, he refused, continuing with his game. In order to discourage the boy from his endeavours, the servant took matters into his own hands by boxing him soundly around the ears. The child, taking umbrage, went home and told his mother what had happened, after which Mary swore along with her mother to do what she could to bring Master Inger to ruin.

It was the servant rather than Inger himself who was to feel Mary's wrath over the treatment of her son. Along with another of Inger's men, the elderly servant was taking corn to market. As they reached the end of the town a black sow appeared, breaking off from grazing on the grass, and followed them as they went on their way. When the men were about a mile outside of Bedford, the sow began to act very strangely; turning and spinning 'as readily as a windmill sail at work.'[4] The horses pulling the cart were spooked by this behaviour, growing more and more agitated until they finally bolted, taking the cart and load but leaving the wheels and axles behind. The men finally caught up with the frightened creatures, calming them with no little effort before reuniting them with the cart and continuing on their way. With the troublesome sow still following at close quarters, they reached their destination without further incident.

After selling the corn at the market, one of the men started the return journey with the cart, while the older servant remained to drink a while with friends. He related the tale of what had happened on their outward journey to much merriment by his companions. Eventually the man said his farewells, making his way on horseback to catch up with his fellow servant. As he spotted the cart in the distance it became apparent that the sow had followed his companion on the way out of town, and as the man upon his horse came level with the cart, the sow did likewise, drawing closer. As before, the horses fell into a frenzy, running off home before the men could stop them. This time only the wheels remained, leaving the men to bring them back to the farm.

After two such incidents it was clear that there was something decidedly amiss regarding the sow. Their suspicions were further raised when the creature was seen going into the house Mary Sutton shared with her mother. When the two men related the events to their master, however, Inger was not convinced, suggesting that they were drunk and dismissing them along with their decidedly wild assertions.

Whether or not Inger gave the matter any further thought, a few days later the same servant was out ploughing, discussing Mary and Mother Sutton with his fellow workers as he went about his task. As he was relating the strange story of their journey to market, a beetle – a large hammer or wooden paddle – struck him on the chest causing him to fall into a trance and his companion to freeze with shock.

Finally the second man recovered his senses enough to go for aid, making his way quickly back to the Inger house. It seemed that the old servant was held in good regard by Inger, who went out to the fields himself to help bring the afflicted man home. Once safely settled the servant was given the best possible care with no expense spared in attempts to make him well again. Despite this, the man continued to suffer and suspicions regarding the cause of his affliction began to form, with whispering about the involvement of Mary Sutton.

With those watching the man almost wishing he would die in order to relieve his terrible suffering, matters grew even stranger. The servant declared that he had seen Mary Sutton in his room at night. With the moon out, he clearly saw her enter by the window, perfectly recognisable and holding her knitting in her hands. Settling herself at the foot of the bed, Mary alternated between working with her needles and staring at the old servant's face. After a time she moved further up the bed towards him before propositioning him most bluntly; if he were to bed her then she would bring an end to his suffering.

Despite being too ill to move or speak before this point, the man suddenly found the strength to convey in no uncertain terms his refusal of her offer. He also took the opportunity to lecture the young woman on the depravity of her behaviour as a whole, pointing out the sin in having not one, but three bastard children to her name. Suitably chastised and realising that the man would not succumb to her advances, Mary made her escape by leaving again through the window. Alone once more the servant called for Inger and informed him of everything that had happened. Inger was somewhat sceptical, wondering if the whole thing had been a feverish fancy but, in order to settle both his servant's mind and his own, he decided to investigate further and sort the matter once and for all.

The following morning, Inger and some of his men went in search of Mary and found her working with the hogs in the fields. After some conversation, Inger revealed the story that his servant had told him. Mary strongly denied having been in the man's room and everything else to do with the tale; when Inger tried to persuade her to go home with him to put his servant's mind at rest, she again refused, telling him firmly that he had no power to make her do as he wished.

Already disposed towards disliking the woman, her behaviour now did little to endear Mary to Inger and without further ado, he had his companions manhandle the young woman onto his horse to carry her away. Mary, understandably none too happy with this development, made things as difficult for the men as possible, wriggling and writhing until she was forcibly held down. After this brutal treatment, she was finally subdued enough to be carried to where the old servant lay.

At his bedside Mary was scratched enough to draw blood from her, in the belief that doing so would break her power over the man. It seemed to work, and the suffering servant appeared to be suddenly and greatly recovered from his sorry state. While this was obviously a good sign, it unfortunately convinced those gathered that Mary was indeed something to do with the strange illness. The man's respite was short-lived; as Mary touched his neck shortly after, he relapsed into the same condition as before.

With events taking place in his very house, it is hardly surprising that Inger's young son became aware of the rumours regarding Mary Sutton and her mother. With the lack of discretion so often displayed by the young, he thought nothing of repeating what he had heard. One day the boy followed Mother Sutton on her way to the mill, throwing stones at the old woman and shouting the accusation of Witch at her. When she returned home she was quick to tell her daughter of the no doubt frightening encounter, and Mary and her mother discussed at length the revenge they would take on the boy.

Whether they had done so before or whether this was a first foray into this particular area of magic was unclear but the two women summoned spirits, named Dick and Jude, to do their bidding. Mary and Mother Sutton let the two demons suck from the teats on their thighs, before sending them out to carry out their plans. It was devastatingly effective as Inger's son was suddenly taken seriously ill, suffering for five days before he died.

Devastated by the loss of his child, Inger confided the whole chain of events to a friend visiting on his way from the North to London. After listening to the terrible story, his visitor asked Inger if he knew who had been the cause of the torment of his servant and death of his son. Inger, perhaps all too glad to have the chance to discuss matters at length, revealed his suspicions regarding Mary and her mother. At this, the visitor made a suggestion; swim the women in the mill pond, and let the water show once and for all whether they were guilty or innocent.

The next day Inger and some of his men again went into the fields where Mary was working. The plan was to bind her to his horse and carry her away, but it was foiled when all the men apart from Inger were suddenly struck lame. Not to be put off, Inger beat Mary with the cudgel he carried. With the young woman stunned, the men recovered enough to help him tie her to the horse. Mary was carried to the mill dam where she was thrown into the water. She sank two feet before rising to the surface again where she floated.

Before the crowd that had gathered by this time, Mary was pulled out of the water and searched for marks by some of the women present. During this examination, a teat was found on her leg, providing further evidence of her witchcraft. Mary was then thrown into the water for a second time, with her thumbs and toes bound together. This time the result was more definite: Mary floated, bobbing about on top of the water for all to see. Even when the rope was shaken and every attempt made to cause her to go under she refused to leave the top of the water, twisting and whirling like a whirlpool, where nothing could induce her to sink.

Once hauled out, Mary remained defiant, denying all the accusations Inger made against her. Taken before a Justice, she continued to plead her innocence, until, in an unexpected twist, it was revealed that her son, Henry Sutton, had given evidence that would fatally turn things against Mary and her mother. The boy had repeated a conversation he had overheard between his mother and grandmother, where they had vowed to get their revenge on Inger and his servant.

Upon hearing of her son's inadvertent betrayal Mary confessed to everything of which she was accused. On the strength of the boy's words, Mother Sutton was also arrested, and the two women were sent to Bedford Gaol. During their incarceration, people were not slow in coming forward with further accusations against the two women and they were found guilty at the following Bedford assizes. Mary and her mother were arraigned on Monday 30 March 1612, and executed the following day by hanging.

The swimming of Mary Sutton in the mill pond at Milton Ernest marked the first documented occasion of a suspected witch undergoing the ordeal in England.[5] The pamphlet detailing the case, which was printed the January after Mary and Mother Sutton's execution, included a step-by-step guide to the process, and did a great deal to promote swimming as a valid test of guilt in subsequent witchcraft cases.[6] Repeated in several later pamphlets, the practice advised by Inger's friend was as follows:

His friend... advised him to take them, or any one of them to his Mill dam, having first shut up the Mill gates that the water might be at highest, and

then binding their arms cross, stripping them into their smocks, and leaving
their legs at liberty, throw them into the water, yet least they should not be
Witches, and that their lives might not be in danger of drowning, let there
be a rope tied about their middles, so long that it may reach from one side of
your dam to the other, where on each side let one of your men stand, that if
she chance to sink they may draw her up and preserve her. Then if she swim,
take her up, and cause some women to search her, upon which, if they find
any extraordinary marks about her, let her the second time be bound, and
have her right thumb bound to her left toe, and her left thumb to her right
toe, and your men with the same rope (if need be) to preserve her, and be
thrown into the water, when if she swim, you may build upon it, that she is a
Witch, I have seen it often tried in the North country.[7]

Although in theory, swimming was carried out to identify a witch, the process could often descend into the sort of mob 'justice' that ended in a lynching.[8] The swimming test, conspicuous by its absence from Scottish witch trials, was common-practice elsewhere across Europe, and found particular favour in Germany where it was popular during the late sixteenth and seventeenth centuries.[9] Another influence that brought the practice to popular attention in England was that of King James I himself. Convinced that witchcraft had been responsible for the difficulties besetting his Queen during her journey to Scotland, his fear spiralled into a personal-vendetta, with seventy people accused over a two-year period. Swimming is referred to in his *Daemonologie*, first published in 1597, where the monarch expressed the view that God had created a supernatural sign that would expose witches for what they really were when they were cast into the water.[10] In 1604, the year after James took the English throne, an act was passed that severely tightened the actions against witches and made the penalties more severe. There is some debate as to whether swimming was already in use in England by the 1590s or not, but one thing is certain: the swimming of Mary Sutton in 1612 and the pamphlet of the following year were instrumental in spreading the practice across the country.[11]

The use of water to establish general guilt or innocence was not without precedent. It was briefly used as a method to try Crown pleas of felony in England between 1166 and 1215, when its use was ended by a decree from the Fourth Lateran Council.[12] This practice was somewhat different however with the ordeal only coming after a guilty verdict had been pronounced by the jury rather than before. Those who passed were often banished from the land, but those who failed were executed.

The ducking of women using a ducking stool is in evidence from 1597. Used to punish unruly, uncontrollable women or scolds, the 'stool' consisted of a chair attached to a long beam of wood. The offending woman would be tied to the chair, which was placed at the edge of the water where she was to be ducked; the beam, on a seesaw-like pivot, allowed it to be lowered into the water and the unfortunate woman submerged.[13]

The practice was discouraged by several writers who saw the downsides to using this method to establish guilt of witchcraft as early as the year of Mary's ordeal. John Cotta, writing in 1612, declared that 'Neither can I believe (I speak it with reverence unto graver judgements) … floating of bodies above the water, or the like, are any trial of a witch.'[14] Such views continued to be expressed in print, and in 1645 a special commission condemned the practice after the excesses of Matthew Hopkins and his fellow witch hunter John Stearne. The process of swimming a witch was still in evidence in an unofficial capacity well into the nineteenth century however, despite increased attempts to curtail it.[15]

Mary's date of birth is unrecorded but Mother Sutton and her husband George had three children: Francis, born in 1578, John in 1580, and Mary, whose baptism is not evident in the registers, either due to gaps or faded/ missing entries. Given the age of her siblings however, it is likely that Mary was between the age of 32 and 40 when she went to her death.[16]

It is interesting to note that there was a second Sutton family living in Milton Ernest at the same time as Mary and her family. Robert Sutton was vicar at the church of All Saints from 1576 until his death in 1611. Although there is no firm evidence that the two families were connected, there are several hints that they might have been so. It is possible that Mary's family followed the family of Robert Sutton into the parish, with the first mention of both appearing in the baptism register for 1578.[17] Perhaps it is coincidental, but Robert Sutton's death occurred just a year before Mary and her mother were brought before the courts. With George Sutton having died in 1605, it could be possible that the removal of this last protection was what precipitated the downfall of two already unpopular women.

The vicar was not without scandal attached to his name either. During 1578 while an archdeacon was visiting Milton Ernest, two of Robert Sutton's own churchwardens – Thomas Jackson and John Church – accused him of cutting down five ash trees in the churchyard, selling them and using the money to buy timber with which to repair his house. The churchwardens were aggrieved that the money hadn't been used to repair the chancel, and there is a strong possibility that Robert Sutton was unpopular amongst at least some of his parishioners.[18] This unpopularity may well have extended outside of Reverend Sutton's immediate family, with Mother and Mary Sutton treated with equal suspicion and dislike.

Following the death of Mary and her mother, the Sutton family seem to have vanished from Milton Ernest.[19] After the death of Robert Sutton, there is no sign of his wife or children having remained, and anyone connected to Mary is gone from Milton Ernest by 1612. The next time the Sutton name appears in Milton Ernest is in the marriage register for 1746, when a George Sutton married Elizabeth Little in January of that year. A daughter, Elizabeth, was born to the couple in the following year, with Susan (1749) and Hannah (1753) following not long after. George himself died in 1755, the same year in which another daughter, Anne, was baptised.[20] Whether there was anyone in the village who remembered the fate of Mary Sutton is unknown, but after nearly a century and a half these probable descendants of Mary and her mother had finally felt that it was safe to return.

Rather than being just an attempt to smear her character, the fact that Mary Sutton's three children were illegitimate is verified by the parish registers for Milton Ernest.[21] It was not just the stain of perceived sexual immorality that brought Mary to the noose however, even as a persistent offender. She was not the only one to have a child out of wedlock by any means; in 1603 for example, Jane Howe is recorded as the illegitimate child of Mary Howe, and whether the term harlot is applied to her as one of loose morals, or with the more innocent meaning of a common servant or female tramp, the child's father is conspicuous by his absence.[22]

The Inger family who played such a prominent role in the fate of Mary and her mother are present in the Milton Ernest parish registers from

1605. That year records the death of not one but two of John Inger's sons; Thomas, buried 2 April, with Edward following just over a month later on 11 May.[23] There is no record of the cause of death, but it is likely that one or both of these sons were those Mary Sutton was accused of harming. There is no record of the ages of Edward or Thomas, nor do we know anything further about them. Given the short distance of time between the deaths it is possible that the same illness carried off both boys, leaving the grieving Ingers with one remaining son, John, born in 1591.[24] A daughter, Margaret, was born in December of that year, and Alice followed in 1608. There is no further record of the Ingers in Milton Ernest after the birth of Alice, and it is unclear where the family went after the execution of Mary and her mother as no trace remains of them in the village. Perhaps they could not bring themselves to stay where they had known such unhappiness, even with the women they blamed for their loss removed.

Mary and her mother would have been guilty of an offence punishable by death under the 1563 Witchcraft Act, as their supposed actions had resulted in the death of Inger's son. Under the 1604 Act passed by James I however, they were guilty on three counts. Along with the death of the boy, they had caused the wasting of John Inger's servant, and also, crucially, were guilty of consorting with evil spirits. Under the new Act, anyone who:

> ... *shall use practise or exercise any Invocation or Conjuration of any evil and wicked Spirit, or shall consult covenant with entertain employ feed or reward any evil and wicked Spirit to or for any intent or purpose...*[25]

... was to be punished by death. The writer of the pamphlet makes it clear that because Mary and her mother summoned Dick and Jude to torment the Inger child, they were both guilty of this and readers would be in no doubt that they had met the end they deserved.

Although prisoner lists do not exist for the year of Mary and her mother's execution, and the record of their trial has not survived, it is likely that they were taken to either the County Gaol in Bedford or the Town Gaol. The former, situated on the corner of Silver Street where it meets the High Street, later housed John Bunyan, of *Pilgrim's Progress* fame, as an inmate. Executions took place further out of town at Gallows Corner on Bromham

Road, last used in 1794, and it is likely that this is where Mary and her mother met their end.

Today, there is little to remind people of the Sutton family in Milton Ernest. The Mill Pond where Mary was swum is still in evidence, but there is little else to show that she and her mother ever existed. Mary's legacy lived on however in the continuation of swimming as a practice and the woodcut depicting the act that is now so familiar to those reading about the history of witchcraft.

Chapter Five

A Servant's Revenge: Joan Flower (1619)

A swearing and blaspheming wretch,
forespeaking sudden death:
and how that neighbours in her looks,
malicious signs did see:
And some affirmed she dealt with Spirits,
and so a Witch might be.

Damnable Practices, 1619

The desire to see the continuation of a family name has been a curious preoccupation of humankind throughout the centuries. Transcending bounds of class and rank, the overwhelming need to produce a living, healthy heir is a phenomenon common in those born both to low estate and high.

Less than a century before this tale begins, England had broken with Rome over the very same matter when Henry VIII's desperation for a son to succeed him drove the king to excessive lengths to achieve this desire. Not too far down the social scale, the matter was only slightly less crucial for the aristocracy where name, reputation, fortune and power all hinged on the delicate matter of childbearing. For the Sixth Earl of Rutland, Francis Manners, and his wife, Cecilia, this need was no less pressing. Thankfully, they could rest safe in the knowledge that they had not one, but two sons. Henry, Lord Roos and Francis the youngest child should have been more than enough to secure the continuation of the Manners line.

The Manners family were, by the time of Francis' succession to the title in 1612, one of the wealthiest and most influential in England. Well-favoured by King James I, a fact highlighted by the King's visit to the Earl's seat of Belvoir Castle in August of that year, Francis Manners seemed to have it all: power, wealth, influence and heirs. It would be a woman with none of those advantages however, who would be blamed for bringing this happy family to its knees with devastating consequences.

No one is quite certain when Joan Flower and her daughters came to work at the castle. It is possible that they were taken on as servants during preparations for the King's visit in 1612, when the household would have required extra staff to cope with the influx of visitors.[1] The tasks given to Joan and her eldest daughter Philippa are unrecorded, but Margaret was given work both inside in the washhouse, and outside with the poultry, along with the added favour of a live-in position. In addition to their enviable roles, it seems that Joan and her daughters were also on good terms with the Earl and his wife, with Joan especially enjoying their confidence and friendship.

Storm clouds were gathering however, as there were those who were not happy with the Flower women. Mutterings and rumours were to be heard in the nearby village of Bottesford where Joan and Philippa lived in a small cottage. The relationship between the castle and village was tight-knit and complex and many of Joan's fellow servants were also her neighbours. In such an atmosphere, discord could easily spread.

There was little Joan's enemies could do while the Flower women were in favour and Joan had the ear of the Earl. The happy arrangement came to an abrupt end however when Margaret was dismissed from her position. From the little evidence available, it seems likely that the young woman was availing herself of the customary perquisites of life in service. Various items were finding their way from the castle to the cottage where Joan and Philippa Flower lived, and the timing and regularity of her visits home suggests that this was probably at her mother's instigation. Although a certain amount might have been tolerated, it appears that the girl overstepped the mark in exploiting the goodwill of the Countess through her light-fingered behaviour.

There were many who would not think that Margaret had cause for complaint as she was, after all, given the extremely generous parting gifts of 40 shillings, a bolster and a mattress of wool. Regardless, the news was not taken well – least of all by Joan Flower, who no doubt relied on the income brought in by her daughter (not to mention the purloined items), to supplement the earnings of Philippa and herself.

Around the same time as Margaret's dismissal, Joan had a quarrel with a Mr Peake. Again, the terms of the disagreement are not known, but when

Joan complained to the Earl, expecting sympathy and redress on her behalf, she was given short shrift; her supposed friend refused to take her side. It must have been galling indeed to find that the tide had turned against her, and Joan was not a woman to be scorned.

Although keeping an outward pretence of friendliness, Joan did not intend to let the matter lie and vowed to do harm to those who had previously been her supporters. Behind closed doors, she cursed the Earl many times, her anger no doubt fuelled by a sense of unfairness and inability to change the situation. This was when matters took a decidedly more fantastical turn. According to the sources, Joan and her daughters were paid a visit by none other than the Devil himself. Whether they had dabbled in witchcraft before this point is not made clear, but the Devil instructed them in the art of bringing punishment to their enemies. Along with this practical help in spells and charms, the Devil also gave Joan the use of several spirits that would do her bidding and aid in the plan to bring down the Earl.

Whoever this devil was, or whether he existed outside of the imagination of the Flower women and those who later testified against them, is unknown. What is certain is that a terrible illness entered the Manners household in 1613. The Earl and Countess experienced periods of sickness throughout this time, but it became starkly apparent that the Manners' children were to suffer the most. Their eldest son, Henry, Lord Roos, sickened badly. The Earl did everything within his power to try to save him, consulting with the highest medical names he could find, but there are some things that money cannot buy, and the boy died later that same year.[2] The household was thrown into mourning and Henry's younger brother Francis became the only remaining male heir to the Rutland name and estate.

Tongues wagged in the village and at the castle alike. It was claimed that Joan kept bad company and her house visited by the most unsavoury of people. One daughter was already known as a thief and it transpired that Philippa was rumoured to have bewitched Thomas Simpson so that he could love only her. A Mr Vavasour, who had previously been a friend, declared he wanted no more to do with Joan, and the Earl and Countess kept their distance, a sign that Joan's household were no longer in favour.

As the popularity of the Flower women continued to wane, the unthinkable happened. Francis, now Lord Roos following his brother's death, also fell sick. A tragic coincidence perhaps, but one that had dire consequences. Quite what pushed the matter over the edge is unclear, but Joan and her daughters were arrested towards the end of 1618. With the unpopular women incarcerated, the floodgates opened in the local community. Locals claimed they had long suspected Joan of being a witch and how, with hindsight, her whole lifestyle supported this belief. Various neighbours were bold enough to confirm that Joan was known to have had encounters with familiar spirits, and complained of the fear they had lived under from the curses and foul words spoken by the woman.

That Joan had bewitched the Earl's children was first whispered, then openly spoken about. Reports claimed that she had ordered Margaret to bring her a glove belonging to the young Lord Henry Roos and, with the item in her possession, she had rubbed it on the back of her cat. This was no ordinary cat however, but a spirit named Rutterkin given to her by the Devil. The glove was then placed in boiling water and, upon its removal, pricked many times. The final part of the ritual was the burial of the glove in the ground, where it would rot, causing the young man to do likewise. Within the week, Henry Roos had fallen ill and eventually died. The same ritual had been performed on the glove of the younger boy, and he too had become sick.

One child Joan was not able to touch was Katherine, the Earl's daughter by his first marriage. A piece of the young woman's handkerchief was obtained by Margaret at her mother's behest, and it was put into hot water and rubbed on the cat as before. Upon trying to send Rutterkin to Katherine however, the cat whined and cried – the spirit had no power to harm the Earl's daughter. Not content with this, Joan then vowed, not only to take away the existing children of the Earl and Countess, but also to ensure that they would have no further offspring. To achieve this, Joan took some wool out of a mattress belonging to the couple along with a pair of gloves she had found, and put them in warm water. The mixture was stirred together with some blood, before the wool and gloves were removed from the water and rubbed on the belly of Rutterkin – with the express purpose of making sure the Countess would never again carry a child.

Joan and her daughters were due to be taken from Bottesford to Lincoln, where they would be held until they faced trial but Joan was fated never to reach their destination. During the journey she declared that she wanted to eat bread in order to prove her innocence.[3] Unfortunately for Joan, she choked and died on the bread and butter given to her, certain evidence to all concerned that she was guilty of the crimes of which she was accused.

Joan was buried at Ancaster having never stood trial, and her daughters were left to travel on to their fate. They were tried at the Lincoln Assizes and, through evidence given against them by both witnesses and each other, they were found guilty and sentenced to death. They were hanged at Lincoln Castle on 11 March, 1619.

The death of Joan and her daughters did little to help the Earl and Countess. Francis, the increasingly poorly Lord Roos, died 5 March, 1620, plunging the continuation of the Manners family into jeopardy and leaving the Earl and his wife grief stricken.[4] Francis Manners was so convinced that Joan and her witchcraft had been responsible for the death of his two sons, that upon his tomb in the Church of St Mary, Bottesford, he had inscribed the words:

In 1608 he married ye lady Cecila Hungerford, daughter to ye Honourable Knight Sir John Tufton, by whom he had two sons, both of which died in their infancy by wicked practices and sorcery.

That the case of the Flower women impacted far more than just those closely involved is very clear, the shock-waves reverberating through the local area. The Reverend Charles Odingsells of nearby Langar preached two sermons in 1619 that dealt with witchcraft, showing that the case had touched more than just the Earl and his family, striking fear into the communities of the Vale of Belvoir.[5]

Joan's exact age is unclear. She is referred to in connection to 'ancient people' in the neighbourhood who were recipients of the generosity of the Earl, but this statement could put her at anything from 50 to 90 based on perceptions of age at the time.[6] There is also no firm indication of the ages of her daughters, and birth records for the three women are unfortunately either lacking, or untraceable in the Bottesford registers.

Exactly where Joan and her family originated from is also unknown, although there were other Flower families in Bottesford and the surrounding area who probably had connections with Joan and her daughters. Thomas Flowar (or Flower) of Bottesford married Elizabeth Fairbane in 1598. They had three children between 1599 and 1602, and it seems that Elizabeth Flower herself died in 1603.[7] Thomas is listed as a gentleman, suggesting that the family had not always been in the dire straits that Joan found herself in. The parish registers of Langar, in Nottinghamshire, list a Henry Flower as marrying Agnes Derbye in 1606, while Mary Flower married William Brockton in 1598. That this line of the family was in Langar from the fifteenth century is evidenced by the 1471 will of a William Flower, and the marriage of a Francis Flower to Mary Darbee in 1614.[8] Langar is only a few miles from Bottesford, and it is possible that the family of Joan's un-named husband originated from here. No other members of the family are mentioned in the account of the Flowers' story however, and it is possible that family, as well as neighbours, readily distanced themselves from the unpopular women.

Wherever they came from, the association of the Flower family with that of the Earl was not a new one. The records of the Duke of Rutland show rewards for the year 1541 including 'Item given upon Shroft Sunday to Flower, of Langar, his servant for bringing two lambs to my Lord Roose and My Lady Talbot'. In 1557, a Mistress Flower was paid her wages under the heading of 'Money disbursed and paid to my Lady's gentlewomen and others for their wages.'[9]

These earlier entries showed just how far the family had fallen by the time of Joan's employment at the castle. The starkest difference is shown in two later entries: one in 1603 when 5 shillings were paid to Mrs Flower's servant in exchange for a cake, and a second in 1615 when a reward was paid to a 'Goodwife Flower' in reward for bringing two hens.[10] It is probable that these both refer to Joan. The change from "Mistress" to 'Goodwife' was significant, showing a reduction in status.[11] This is most likely due to a change in marital status, namely the death of Joan's husband.

There is no death record for a possible candidate in the Bottesford registers. Nevertheless, there is speculation that John Flower from Hucknall, also mentioned in the Rutland accounts might have been Joan's husband.[12] Also of note is a marriage between a Henry Flower and Joan Johnson of Ashby Magna in 1588. This would suggest a birth date for Joan of around 1560, putting her at just shy of 60 years of age at her death.

It is clear that Joan was not well liked in the village of Bottesford. She was referred to as 'a monstrous malicious woman, full of oaths, curses and imprecations irreligious.'[13] Her living was lewd, her reputation bad, she kept company with those best avoided, and her daughters were not much better. In appearance, it was said that she was hollow eyed and wild – perhaps a reality, or perhaps exaggerated in order to express the fact that inner wickedness was shown outwardly on a person. In her book *Witches* covering the Belvoir case, Tracy Borman puts forward the interesting theory that those men listed as eventually quarrelling with Joan – Mr Peake, Mr Vavasour and perhaps others – were actually involved with Joan sexually, adding more weight to the suggestion that she was deeply immoral and corrupting those around her.[14]

That the Earl took the charge of witchcraft seriously has already been demonstrated. Further evidence is found in the Earl's accounts, which show that, on 16 March 1619, a Mr Jephson was paid £20 for charges in prosecuting the witches, and that a further £20 was spent on the Earl's journey to Lincoln that same month.[15] It seems that Francis Manners and his brother George Manners questioned Joan's daughters and, however painful this might have been, what they said convinced him of the guilt of these former friends.

Although Joan was not present at the trial of her daughters, there was much revealed there that adds to the picture of the older woman. For instance, it was at the trial that rumours regarding the obtaining and burying of the children's gloves were corroborated by both Margaret and Philippa, who said they had done so on their mother's bidding. Through this and other statements, they not only confirmed what was said about Joan, but also accused and implicated one another, perhaps too distraught by this time to do anything else.

Other local women also spoke out against them. Joan Wilmott related a conversation with Joan Flower where the old woman had complained that the Earl of Rutland had badly treated both her and her daughters, and because she could not harm the Earl himself, she had turned on his children. Joan Wilmott went on to relate how she had met Joan and Margaret Flower about a week before the old woman's arrest. The meeting took place on Blackborrow Hill and before they went on to Joan Flower's house, where

Joan Wilmott claims to have seen two spirits: one like a rat and one like an owl. Joan Flower told her that the spirits had said she would never be burned or hanged, a fact which had proven to be correct. Joan Wilmott also told how Joan had picked up some earth and spat into it before working it with her fingers and put it into her purse, repeating that although she couldn't hurt the Earl she could get to him through doing ill to his children.[16]

The Earl and those who had spoken against the Flower women clearly believed that they were guilty. And it seemed that Margaret and Philippa did too; confirming and confessing to the events already related by others. Joan, on the other hand, was a different matter; despite the rumours regarding what she had said and done, Joan did not confess to anything after her arrest and died while attempting to prove her innocence.

That she spoke heated words against the Earl and his wife is not in doubt; that she considered the dismissal of Margaret as unfair, along with the refusal of the Earl to take her part, was more than enough reason to have her cursing his name. It is also possible that, given the corroboration of the many statements against her, Joan did indeed perform something that she saw as witchcraft. It was, after all, one of the very few modes of redress open to someone of Joan's social status against someone as powerful as the Earl of Rutland. Whatever the case, Joan maintained her innocence until her dying breath, choking on bread.

Joan's request to be tried that way was by no means unknown. The practice, known as *corsned* in Anglo-Saxon times, was, according to the Oxford English Dictionary:

> *In Old English law, the morsel of trial, a piece of bread of about an ounce weight consecrated by exorcism (panis conjuratus) which an accused person was required to swallow as a trial of his guilt or innocence.*[17]

The original practice was a great deal more complex than Joan's version, but the idea behind it was the same. It has been suggested that originally the consecrated Eucharist would have been used, then changed to normal bread once it was not so easy to get hold of that used for Communion. The Lord's Prayer would be written on the bread by the priest, and ten pennyweights of both bread and cheese would be weighed out. A complex ritual followed, but eventually the bread and cheese would be placed, at the same moment, in the mouth of the accused whilst words were spoken, as both a conjuration and prayer of exorcism. God would be called upon to search the heart of the accused in order to discover whether they be innocent or guilty and to show this by either allowing the food to pass through or not.[18] Convulsions, paleness of face and the ultimate sign of choking were all clear signs of guilt, but if innocent, the bread would nourish the person being tried and pass through normally.[19]

It could be said that either Joan was utterly convinced of her own innocence of the crimes of which she was accused or else she was very confident that her diabolical master would not let any harm come to her. But perhaps, instead, she was simply a terrified old woman willing to try anything to get out of the situation in which she found herself. Whatever the case, those who denounced her would have concluded that her fate was the final proof that Joan Flower was the witch everyone suspected her to be.

Despite the seemingly clear-cut case against the Flower women, it appears that doubts were raised after the event regarding their guilt and opinion continued to fluctuate throughout the centuries. Two contemporary sources survive recording the case, a pamphlet: *The Wonderful Discoverie of the Witchcraft of Margaret and Phillip* [sic] *Flower, daughters of Joan Flower, near Belvoir Castle*, and a ballad, *Damnable Practises* both written not long after the women's deaths.[20] These were both greatly weighted in the favour of the Earl and his family, and it is highly likely that either the Earl, or a close associate, was responsible for the printing of both accounts. The careful wording, and portrayal of the Earl as just and charitable, could perhaps be taken as a protest too far, the need to prove the women guilty evident.[21] In a later book we find the assessment that: 'However we may deplore the ignorance of the times, these unhappy women could not be said to be innocent; as, from the depositions of others, and their own examinations and confessions, there could be no doubt of their intentional guilt. In short, they believed themselves witches.'[22] However, the arrest of three other local women not long after the Flower women could be a sign of an attempt to prove that their arrest and execution were warranted. Joan Willimot, Ellen Green and Anne Baker were accused of helping Joan and her daughters, and also of witchcraft in their own right. Although it appears that they were eventually released unscathed, it could be argued that this 'proof' that witchcraft was rife, and that Joan had been involved, was intended to silence those who might have their suspicions against the justness of what had been carried out.[23] The final line of the pamphlet also bears mentioning because, although in Latin, it hides a potential clue that things were not as they seemed. Translated as 'if only I could find out the truth as easily as I can show up the lies!' this might suggest that the writer was a little sceptical, despite what he had been commissioned to write.[24]

It has been suggested that there was a more sinister reason behind the fates of Joan and her daughters than belief in their guilt. George Villiers, Duke of Buckingham from 1623, had his eye on Katherine Manners as a potential bride. The proposed match was beset with troubles from the start, not least of all Katherine's Catholicism, her would-be husband's unrealistic financial expectations, and the strong opinions of family on both sides. It was clear, however, that Villiers was keen for Katherine to become his wife and that if the Earl's sons were out of the way, Katherine would bring a much larger amount of land and money to her husband. It was, therefore, in Villier's interests to have her brothers quietly removed. It has thus been mooted that the future Duke conspired to have the younger of the Manners boys killed, with the Flowers women being unfortunate scapegoats and paying the price for his ambition.[25]

Whatever his role in the matter, Villiers had his wish, and on 16 May 1620, he and Katherine Manners were finally married, the bride taking with her a dowry of £10,000 up front and between £4–£5,000 a year to follow. The couple had four children that may have caused her grieving step-mother great envy before Buckingham's assassination in 1628.[26]

There were several elements in the case of Joan Flower that were unusual for the time. Although often linked in witchcraft trials on the Continent, the idea of witches causing infertility was not a common one in English cases at this point, and witches were not generally blamed for interfering with sexual relations.[27] While barrenness caused by witchcraft was rare, being unable to produce much-longed for children was not. A quarter of all married couples were childless, with infertility accounting for around twelve per cent of those marriages that did not have children.[28] For the Earl of Rutland it was not just a case of seeing his name die out. If he had no male heir then his daughter, Katherine, would inherit the lands that were attached to the Roos barony thus becoming an heiress in her own right and causing the break-up of the Manners' lands.[29] This was something that the Earl, after working so hard to rebuild the fortunes of his family, was keen to avoid.

This desperation explains the unsuccessful actions taken to conceive another child after the death of their son Francis. Barrenness was regarded as a distinctly female malady. The Countess had proven that she could bear children, but she was now considered unable to do so in the aftermath of the Flower incident. Thus, efforts to change the situation were focused on the Countess, with entries in the account books showing that she made several trips in connection with her condition. One such journey was to Tunbridge Wells, in Kent, the waters there known for their restorative and curative powers.[30] This was no small undertaking, the visit lasting over a week with the final bill coming in at £100. There were also charms to cure impotence within marriage in contemporary magical books, but there is no evidence that these were sought out in the case of the Earl and Countess.[31] The couple had no further children, the cures the Countess sought proving sadly ineffective.

There were several ways that one could come under the spell of a witch; being cursed verbally, being touched by the witch, or being caught by the evil eye. Another matter that made Joan Flower's case unusual was the use of physical aids in order to bewitch a victim. This could be the burning of a piece of paper with the name written on for instance, or a wax figure of the person who was to be harmed. In the case of the Manners children, it was the burying of a glove that was the cause of their bewitchment and gave Joan power over them. This was not a common feature of English witchcraft cases at the time.[32]

There are few traces left of Joan and her family today. There is a cottage in Bottesford that is known as the witch's house and is believed in local lore to be linked with the tale of Joan and her daughters. It is considered unlikely that this was the house where Joan Flower lived and where Margaret brought her ill-gotten gains, however nice a story it might make.[33] The Flower surname is present in Bottesford through both the seventeenth and eighteenth centuries, and the name appeared in the surrounding areas.[34] There is also the inscription and two sad figures on the Rutland tomb in St Mary's Church, Bottesford for visitors to see today.

Joan features in two novels, the first Hilda Lewis' *The Witch and the Priest*.[35] As the protagonist, Joan is presented as a sympathetic figure despite her abominable crime, appearing as a ghost to talk with one of the clergy who, the book posits, could, or should, have saved her soul. She also appears in a smaller role in *A Cavalier Stronghold* by Mrs Chaworth Muster written in 1890 and set in the area.[36] There was also an opera called Rutterkin, the name of course taken from Joan's cat that was performed in 1972 and 1995 in the local area.

Where Joan finally rests is unrecorded. The pamphlet says she was buried at Ancaster, where the parish church of St Martin's dates back to the Norman period and was built on the site of a Roman temple. The parish registers are unhelpful in the quest for Joan as they only date back to 1722, and although the Bishop's Transcripts are available from 1562, there is no record of Joan's burial there.[37] Although her final resting place must remain unknown, what cannot be doubted is the impact Joan Flower, a poor servant, had on the powerful and mighty Manners family. Through her real or imagined revenge on the Earl of Rutland, she has passed into history as one of England's most terrible witches.

Chapter Six

The Ipswich Witch: Mary Lakeland (1645)

Several other things she did, for all which she was by Law condemned to
die, and in particular to be burned to death, because she was the death of her
husband, as she confessed; which death she suffered accordingly.
The Laws Against Witches and Conjuration – 1645

The idea that witches were burnt for their crimes is one of the most
enduring and steadfastly held misconceptions in the history of
English witchcraft. Conflated with the burnings for heresy and
treason under the reigns of the Tudors and with the addition of tales that
have passed into legend, one might be forgiven for thinking that England
had vast quantities of witches who went to the flames.[1]

It might come as a surprise therefore to learn that, although burning was
common-place on the Continent and in Scotland, only a small handful of
witches in England met with a fiery fate and even then for crimes other than
the witchcraft of which they were also accused.[2]

Of the few accused of witchcraft that did meet this gruesome end, the
case of Mary Lakeland or Lackland of Ipswich is the best substantiated.
Living in the parish of St Clements, the newer maritime area of the town
just outside the old town wall, she was, according to the pamphlet in which
her fate is recorded, a deeply devout woman and a 'professor of religion' who
attended the town's weekly sermons. She had also been, as she admitted in
her 'confession', a witch for nearly twenty years.[3]

According to Mary, the first time the Devil came to her was in that grey
area between sleep and wakefulness, when dreams can seem real and, for a
few moments, reality uncertain. Her diabolical visitor spoke to her in a voice
that sounded hollow, before promising that she should have whatever she
wanted if only she would agree to serve him. How Mary felt at this can only
be guessed, but after several similar visitations, she consented. The Devil

was clever indeed, however, because he did not push Mary too far. She was not asked to deny either her faith or Christ; the Devil knew that because of her religious nature, she would not consent to such an arrangement. The bargain was sealed by the Devil cutting her palm with his claw, using her blood to write the pact between them. In return he gave Mary three imps, or familiars, in the form of two small dogs and a mole.

With the Devil behind her and these imps to do her bidding, Mary made good use of her new status. She bewitched her husband, the barber John Lakeland, causing him to suffer from an illness before he finally died. She also had several debts that were causing her problems. One of these was 12 shillings owed to a Mr Lawrence, who had asked for the money to be repaid to him. Either unable or unwilling to repay the debt, Mary sent one of the dogs to him, tormenting both the man and his child to death.[4] A maid of Mrs Jennings' household was also rash enough to ask for the repayment of a shilling Mary had borrowed from her, a request that, along with the further offence of refusing to lend Mary a needle, led to her suffering the same torment as the Lawrence family.

Mary went on to send one of her imps to John Beale who had, at one time, shown interest in her grand-daughter. How far the romance had progressed is unclear, but when Beale ceased his attentions, Mary took umbrage on the young woman's behalf, sending her familiar to burn the man's new ship. Not content with that, she instructed the imp to further torment the fickle suitor, with the intent of taking his life as she had done with the Lawrence family and the maid. Although Beale did not die, he was left to live in the greatest of misery; half of his body rotting and withering away before his very eyes.

There were others who were also to come under attack. Another man with an interest in shipping also fell victim to Mary's ire, and she cast away a vessel belonging to Henry Reade, killing both the unfortunate owner and his crew, though it is not certain what this man had done to cause Mary to seek such revenge. Thomas Holgrave, like John Beale, also suffered wasting in his body, the outcome of which is unknown.

There is no record of the date of Mary's arrest or the exact events that led up to it. Once she was arrested however she was held at Ipswich gaol.[5] The indictments drawn up against Mary were as follows:

For witchcraft and murder of Elizabeth Aldham.

For witchcraft and murder of William Lawrence.

For witchcraft and murder of Sarah Clarke.

For casting away Henry Reade's ship and murdering the said Reade and divers persons unknown.

For felony and witchcraft and traitorously murdering of John Lakeland her husband.

For felony and witchcraft and wasting the body of John Beale.

For felony and witchcraft and wasting the body of Thomas Holgrave.

For felony and witchcraft and nourishing of evil spirits.

For witchcraft and burning the ship of John Beale.[6]

The nourishing of evil spirits alone was enough to convict Mary and condemn her to death under the 1604 Witchcraft Act, and with several counts of murder included she had little hope. Despite pleading innocent during her trial at the Moot Hall, Ipswich, she was found guilty on 2 August of each charge, along with several others also being tried for witchcraft related crimes. As witchcraft was decreed a felony in England, those found guilty of the crime were punished in the same way as any other felony, by hanging. However, having caused the death of her husband, Mary was found guilty of petty treason and sentenced to burn.

Mary's execution took place on Tuesday 9 September 1645, probably where the execution of heretics and traitors took place in the south-east corner of the Cornhill.[7] Alice Denham, also condemned at the same time as Mary, was said to have been paraded through the streets before being hanged.[8]

There is no record of what happened at the execution itself, but details of a burning of someone guilty of felony can be found in a pamphlet of the time and it is likely that Mary suffered in a similar fashion:

Then the Executioner setting her in a pitch barrel, bound her to the stake, and placed the straw and Faggots about her; whereupon she lifting her eyes towards Heaven, desired all that were present to pray for her; and the Executioner putting fire to the straw, she cried out, Lord Jesus have mercy on my soul; and after the fire was kindled she was heard to shriek out terribly some five or six several times.[9]

Although of little consolation to Mary, one of her supposed victims actually recovered. On the very day of Mary's execution, John Beale began to show signs of improvement. He had been suffering with a large bunch of flesh on his thigh that none of his doctors had been able to remove or explain; it was said to be in the shape of a dog, a fact that confirmed to people that it was of unnatural origin and further evidence of Mary's influence. This lump, now that Mary was dead, suddenly came away of its own accord. Not only that, but a sore that had been present since Mary's imp had visited him and had refused to heal, now started to improve and for the first time in a year and a half it was hoped that he might actually recover. As there is no death record for a John Beale in the years directly following Mary's death, one might hope that he continued to live happily for quite some time.

As in so many cases, biographical details for Mary and her family are sadly lacking. The pamphlet that records the details of her case does not reveal how old she was, although we are told that she has been practising witchcraft for the space of twenty years and was old enough to have a grand-daughter of marriageable age.[10] In 1595, Mary was living with her husband John, a barber, in the parish of St Stephens, and by the 1620s the couple had moved to the St Clements area of the town. It appears that by 1637, John was old and sick because his son, George, was let off paying the 1d a week rates to help contribute towards his ailing father's upkeep.[11] There are several John Lakelands listed for burials in the first half of the seventeenth century in Ipswich, but it is most likely that John Lakeland was buried 26 August, 1638, in the church of St Clements.

The death of her husband would have left the widowed Mary in a diminished position both financially and socially, which explains the tales of debts recounted at her trial. It seems that the family were not always in such dire straits that they would quibble over a shilling though because both John Lakeland and his son George are listed as 'Freemen' of the city. This referred to those who had 'inherited or acquired by adoption, purchase or apprenticeship the rights of a citizen.'[12] There were several benefits to this status: a freeman could be self-employed within the town, was eligible for business protection, and was exempt from the payment of tolls. A freeman could also take part in the administration side of the borough, having an influence on the quality and pricing of goods within it. They also had the right to vote.

There were four ways in which a man might enter the lists of the freemen. John Lakeland's route was servitude or apprenticeship, his master being listed as William Bate. For this, he would have to have been born in wedlock, be at least 21 years of age and have been indentured to an existing freeman for seven years. Interestingly, a freeman could either be male or female, although Mary is not recorded as having achieved this status or having a trade.[13]

There is no record of Mary's marriage to John Lakeland, or of her maiden name, so it is unclear as to who her family might have been. We know, however, that she had at least one son, the aforementioned George, and at least one grandchild, rejected by John Beale to his cost. As for the Lakelands, a Robert Lackland married in St Clements in 1622, whilst in the St Nicholas parish of Ipswich there was the family of Theophilius Lakeland.[14] It is not too much of a stretch to consider that both families may have been relations of Mary's husband, John, and therefore related to Mary through marriage.

Mary was known to be devout, but also, if the accusations against her are to be believed, capable of seeking vengeance against those with whom she was unhappy. Daniel Defoe, writing in 1726, refers to the case in *The Political History of the Devil,* stating that 'being very poor, and withall of devilish passionate, cruel and revengeful Disposition before, used to wish she had it in her Power to do such and such mischievous Things to some that she hated.'[15] As far as Defoe was concerned, Mary met the fate she deserved. Mary's reputation was still low well over a century later when in *A New Guide to Ipswich* (1842) it is related that in 1645, Ipswich had been plagued by a 'notorious witch.' This source believed her to be the last sorceress in Ipswich for whom a confession existed.[16] Craig Cabell, a more recent biographer of Matthew Hopkins, speculates that, at the very least, Mary must have been a wicked woman at heart, even if she were not guilty of the actual crimes for which she was condemned, before erroneously stating that as she never tried to take back her confession then she was very probably guilty.[17]

Although the pamphlet account of Mary's case is punctuated throughout with references to how she confessed her guilt, other documentary sources maintain that she pleaded not guilty.[18] Although a less commonly cited source, the Ipswich Borough Records for the time states that for each charge she 'pleads not guilty' and as there is no other record of her having made a confession after this point apart from the pamphlet, with its decidedly anti-Mary leanings, it is debatable whether Mary ever actually confessed to her supposed crimes.[19]

Whether she confessed or not made no difference to her fate. The words of those who gave evidence and the deliberations of Oliver Reeve, William Bull, Joseph Ward and Stephen Johnson (paid ten pounds each for their work), secured the guilty verdict against her.[20]

Under the 1604 Witchcraft Act, Mary was found guilty under two counts: consulting with evil spirits in the form of a familiar, and using witchcraft to waste or kill the body of another. The pamphlet account tells us that '…for all which she was by Law condemned to die, and in particular to be burned to death, because she was the death of her husband, as she confessed; which death she suffered accordingly.'[21] There are no other details of Mary's death or how she faced it; the mood of the crowd and those watching can only be imagined.

Although English witches were not burnt for the crime of witchcraft, as already noted, burning *was* the standard punishment for those found guilty of treason. Mary was burnt because she was found guilty of killing her husband, a form of treason known as 'petty-treason' which carried the death penalty. According to the 1351 Treason Act, Petty Treason was defined as the murder of one's lawful superior – a servant killing his master or, as in Mary's case, a wife killing her husband, the head of the household and ruler of those within it, including his spouse. Under the Act, men found guilty of the crime were sentenced to drawing and hanging, whilst women were condemned to death by burning.[22]

The letter of the law was harsher against women than men when it came to violent acts. An act of violence by a man towards his wife was considered 'due correction', whereas a woman was considered dangerously insubordinate. Not only that, wives who murdered their husbands – violently or otherwise – were more vulnerable to conviction because their acts often appeared pre-meditated.[23] Despite this, figures show that conviction of women for capital crimes was on the low side, and of those convicted, the number of executions actually carried out were lower still.[24] Even where petty treason was concerned, it was rare for the death sentence to be passed because women were seen as less likely to disturb public order, and therefore dealt with more leniently.[25]

As for the crime of witchcraft itself, the numbers for Ipswich are well documented and it can be seen that, even within this group, Mary stood out. not only for being convicted, but for the fact that she was executed at all. There were nineteen cases between 1581 and 1645, during which time twice as many were acquitted as convicted, which makes Mary's fate all the more perplexing. The largest number of suspects, eight in total, were tried in 1645.[26] Two were found not guilty, whilst one case was counted 'unproven', with the accused having to find sureties for good behaviour. The outcome against another is unknown beyond pleading not guilty like the rest. The remaining four were found guilty: two acquitted of major charges and thus sentenced to a year's imprisonment and four appearances in the pillory and one was hanged. Leaving Mary alone to go to the flames.

Mary's case was, therefore, somewhat remarkable. This fact has been explained with several theories over the years, although it could be argued that none is entirely satisfactory. One of the simplest suggestions is that Mary was a quarrelsome, trouble-making old woman who had caused enough disruption and unrest amongst her neighbours that the town authorities wanted her removed.

The borrowing of money from Lawrence and the maid implies that Mary's need for money, and the refusal to pay it back, was likely due to an inability to do so. Poverty stricken widows were a problem for the town in general, with their numbers on the increase throughout the seventeenth century. Mary's parish was most particularly affected and in 1597 St Clements had the second largest number of poor of all Ipswich parishes.[27] While they did their best to scrape together an existence on money earned picking oakum, and spinning or knitting, ultimately women like Mary added to the amount of poor relief paid out each year and executing her would have meant one less to be paid for.[28]

Then there is, of course, the fact that people believed her to be a witch. It is not known who first spoke against Mary or the course of events that led to her arrest, but it would not be hard to imagine friends or family of one of her supposed victims taking the first step to report Mary to the authorities. Through accounts of her case, a picture is painted of Mary terrorising her community, meting out dire punishments to those who dared to question or confront her. Perhaps she had spoken out about her desire to have revenge on the unfortunate John Beale or railed against those who had tried to call in their debts, giving those who disliked and feared her an opportunity to have her removed.

Keeping Mary alive on public charity was costly, as was the solution of keeping her out of the way by indefinite imprisonment, hardly ideal at the cost to the town of 3 pence per prisoner per day.[29] This doesn't, however, explain satisfactorily why they would burn her rather than use the noose, as it cost £1 to hang a witch in 1646, compared to the £3 3s 6d it cost to burn her.[30] Mary was already guilty of a crime punishable by death through covenanting with familiar spirits so there would have been little need to push for the more expensive punishment. The whole matter of witchcraft prosecution itself was another added expense; only a week before Mary's execution, it was passed that the costs of searching, watching and prosecuting those suspected as witches within Ipswich was to be met by the people of the town.[31] It could be argued that it was decided to make an example of Mary, or that she needed to be removed for another reason.

Another explanation is that Mary was indeed targeted, not for witchcraft, but for her religious leanings. The religious life of the town was strictly governed; in the weekly flow of routine, inhabitants of the town were expected to attend compulsory lectures twice a week, on Wednesday and Friday, lasting three hours each.[32] David Jones argues that, through her religious dedication, Mary might have emerged as the head of a group of fellow widows who went one step further than just enjoying the town's weekly sermons, taking it upon themselves to discuss and speak out about what was said. There had been a group of such widows in the town for years and records show them being harassed by the authorities on more than one occasion. There have been arguments that Mary was in fact a puritan dissident who criticised the town authorities.[33] In the carefully controlled and monitored environment of seventeenth century Ipswich, it is possible that Mary's activities came to the attention of the authorities and raised concern. Perhaps she had over stepped the mark in her 'professing' of religion, and it is possible that she may have been a member of one of the radical sects in operation in the town at the time. She may possibly have been a Baptist; there had been recent steps taken by the authorities to restrain them.[34]

Taking this further, Jones speculates that Mary might have quarrelled with the town lecturer, the best paid official in the town and the deliverer of the weekly sermons that Mary so devoutly attended. The removal of Mary was therefore part of a conspiracy, a personal vendetta to remove a troublesome woman. Jones argues that the Mr Lawrence, whom Mary acted against, was actually Matthew Lawrence, who held the position of Lecturer and that it was his son whom Mary was accused of killing.[35] Although the Lawrence family mentioned in Mary's case may have been related to Matthew Lawrence, it is unlikely to have been the lecturer himself, because the pamphlet against Mary states that her victim died and Matthew Lawrence, happily for him, died at the age of fifty-three in 1653, eight years after Mary met her fate.[36] More plausible candidates are William Lawrence, who was buried on 2 July, 1643 in St Clements, with Samuel Lawrence, possibly his son, buried 11 July, 1641.

It is likely that a combination of the above factors, along with the situation in Ipswich and the general fear of witchcraft and religious dissidence led to Mary's fate. She may also have come to the attention of the authorities either through her own outspokenness, or someone speaking out against her.

The most extraordinary and least likely explanation for Mary's fate was that, religious views aside, she was acting as a Royalist informant. England was a country at war with itself, the climate of suspicion and intrigue fostered by the Civil War bubbling over on a local level. The men who testified against Mary were terrified not only of witches, but also the secret plots of the feared Royalists. It has been argued that, in this hotbed of unrest and suspicion, Mary was working against the cause of good and using her powers to help the Royalist cause. The idea that Mary may have been working for the Royalists became popularised by Richard Deacon in his biography of Matthew Hopkins, the infamous 'Witchfinder General'. Deacon references a document known as *The Tendring Witchcraft Revelations*, which states that: 'Hopkins…went to Ipswiche especially to examine this suspected informer of the Royalist Lady Whorwood,' implying that this informer was none other than Mary Lakeland.[37] Admitting that there was nothing in the trial to suggest she was involved in politics or intrigue, he nevertheless posed the hypothesis that the motive to burn Mary could have been political, as she was the only one to burn from that assize. He also makes the case that there is firm evidence that Hopkins was involved in Mary's trial.[38]

Lady Jane Whorwood, the loyal supporter of Charles I, was instrumental in smuggling gold and information to the beleaguered monarch, as well as assisting in two failed escape attempts. There is, however, no evidence other than Deacon's word that Mary had any connection with her, and although still often quoted by historians, it is now established that Deacon's book and the document it is supposedly based upon, was nothing but an elaborate hoax.[39]

The mooted involvement of Matthew Hopkins in Mary's trial is also suspect as the 'firm evidence' Deacon refers to is lacking. It has been suggested that, as Hopkins had connections to the shipping industry, John Beale, the man who had so rashly spurned Mary's grand-daughter, had called upon him to do away with the problem of a jilted and unwanted Grandmother-in-law.[40] This is pure speculation however because outside of Richard Deacon's inventions, Hopkins and Stearne were never directly cited as being involved in the witchcraft cases at Ipswich. There is likely to have been some kind of connection however because the same group that backed Hopkins and his partner in their work across Suffolk and Norfolk was also behind the prosecution of those involved in the Ipswich cases.[41] There is also the suggestion that Matthew Hopkins himself might have been the author, or at least the driving force, behind the pamphlet that contains Mary's case.[42]

Although Hopkins' direct involvement in Mary's particular case is questionable, her trial and execution took place during England's most well-documented and well-known 'witch hunt', i.e. 'a sustained persecution over a wide area, orchestrated by people calling themselves witch-finders.'[43] There was no other period in English history like the period of the civil wars, nor one that caused so great an upheaval. A time when both government and religion were overturned; the monarch, in the person of Charles I, removed and finally executed; the House of Lords abolished; the Church of England losing its power and its liturgy done away with.[44] In such charged times it has been suggested that witches became scapegoats for worldly ills and a convenient 'enemy' to blame for otherwise minor vexations, a means of taking back control from forces beyond the ken of those who lived in fear. Astrological forecasts for the year had been bad from the start, and had been borne out by what actually occurred; a poor harvest, coupled with unrest and less than favourable weather conditions. Maxwell-Stuart argues that there is little evidence to support this theory; the patches of the worst plague, and famine and climate conditions did not coincide with a sharp increase in prosecutions for witchcraft in England.[45] He also points out that people tended to blame state officials for problems, not witches.[46] So, however satisfying it may be for us in the modern era to blame superstition and simple-minded folk for witch-hunts at times of societal stress, it does not appear as though Mary was a lightning rod for popular fear and confusion in the Civil Wars.

The pact Mary made with the devil, signed with her own blood, was something of a new development in witchcraft trials and also has links with the situation of the time. Previous to this, although well-known on the Continent, the main focus in English trials had been on maleficium, and where an agreement existed it was in verbal rather than written form. Mary's case marked one of the first instances of the idea of the written pact, as 'then he stroke his claw (as she confessed) into her hand, and with her blood wrote the Covenants.'[47] The pamphlet which contains the tale of Mary's fate also states that:

> *The Witch dealeth rather by a friendly and voluntary conference or agreement between him (or her) and the Devil or Familiar, to have his or her turn served, and in lieu thereof the Witch giveth (or offereth) his or her soule, blood, or other gift unto the Devil.*[48]

There were clear parallels between the devilish pact and the two covenants that had recently come into English legislation, with an unmissable connection to the importance of oaths and covenants at the time.[49] Although there was no evidence of written pacts with the Devil until Hopkins came on the scene in the 1640s, once in the driving seat, Hopkins managed to convince twenty or so women to confess that they had signed documents to the Devil.[50]

There are claims that Mary Lakeland did not entirely leave Ipswich on that day in 1645. In the area where her husband John had his barbershop, there is now, coincidentally, the Lakeland Store in which there have been rumours of ghostly goings on. The Lakeland Store is situated in the Butter Market and it has been reported that many strange things have been experienced by staff members. Flower arrangements have been moved and altered when no one was in the shop. Items have been hidden only to reappear again without any sign of the cause. One member of staff found herself temporarily shut in the cellar. There was also the case of a locked cabinet which, when opened, showed clearly that items within it had been moved around, the marks in the dust betraying movement of some kind.[51] The shop is in the Ancient House, and is located on the corner between St Stephen's Lane and the Butter Market. Built in 1597, the building has gone through much change and restoration since the days of Mary Lakeland, but maybe, just maybe, there is some truth in the rumours that she is, for now, there to stay.

Chapter Seven

A Woman of Ill-Repute: Anne Wagg (1650)

Slipshod and puerile as the statements are, and wholly illogical in their reasoning, they are just as strong as many that were followed by the capital sentence, so we should think there is little doubt that Anne Wagg was burnt to death on evidence that now-a-days would not even convict a poacher.
Three Centuries of Derbyshire Annals – John Charles Cox

Although not at the foreground of the Civil War, Derbyshire was of critical strategic importance during the conflict. Situated between three Royalist strongholds and Charles I's base in Oxford, it was of paramount importance that the county did not pass into Royalist hands; the linking of the King's supporters would have proved disastrous for the Parliamentarian cause.[1] Despite escaping the main brunt of battle, there were still many deaths attributable not only to the fighting, but also the associated effects of famine and disease; out of a population of around 60,000, 1,500 people (1 in 30) died between 1642 and 1651.[2]

On 19 May 1649, England was officially declared a 'Commonwealth and Free State.' This did not necessarily lead to more toleration; on the contrary, the way in which people were to live was more closely regulated than ever.[3] It was expected that people would behave and think according to tightly held views, and those who did not would transgress at their peril.

This is most certainly the case with the story of Anne Wagg, a woman accused of witchcraft in the village of Ilkeston, Derbyshire, in 1650. The story officially began on 18 June, 1650 when Francis Torrat, the local baker, stood before Gervase Bennett, Esquire, Justice of the Peace for Derby, and accused Anne of witchery and causing harm to himself and others. His opening statement was that Anne was well known as a witch in the village where they lived and had been suspected as such for many years. His own personal grounds for complaint were that, three years previously, Anne Wagg had spoken unfavourably about himself and his wife. On what, exactly, there is no record – perhaps there had been a falling out, or maybe it was to do with the recorded fact that Torrat, along with other bakers in the village, was renowned for charging over the fixed price for bread, an offence for which he was regularly fined at the local manor court sessions. Whatever the cause, the damning words were spoken to the Torrats' servant, Elizabeth Parkson, who then repeated the insult to her master and mistress.

The following Sunday, Torrat and his wife were on their way to church with their maid when Anne Wagg stepped forward to block their path. Whether she had been waiting to accost them or just happened to be entering the church at the same time is unclear, but whatever the case she frowned at the maid in such a manner that the whole party were greatly unsettled before moving on their way. The matter might have been forgotten, but soon after Elizabeth Parkson fell ill and found she could not move; the incident with Anne came swiftly to mind and it was agreed by all concerned that Anne was to blame.

With the girl being so ill, she was moved from her usual bed to one in the same room as Torrat and his wife. The household settled for bed, but at nine o'clock the maid called out for help, deeply distressed. Despite being awake, neither Mr or Mrs Torrat were able to move or answer her until something had leapt from the maid's bed. When Torrat could finally speak, the maid demanded to know if he had not seen the cat; it is unclear if Torrat actually admitted to seeing the creature, but he was adamant that he and his wife could not move until the animal had been declared to have left the room. When Torrat finally went to her, the maid was in terrible distress, crying and finding it hard to breathe.

Either on the same occasion or some days later, the same maid recalled the popular belief that the placing of tongs in the fire meant that a witch would be unable to leave the room. Accordingly this was put to the test; Anne (or perhaps a cat that happened to be in the house – the sources are unclear) was in the house and the tongs were set in the fire. As predicted, Anne was unable to leave until the tongs were removed, proof enough to all that she was to blame for what had befallen Elizabeth Parkson.

Torrat concluded his evidence with the assertion that, more recently, William Fox, the vicar of Ilkeston since 1633, had also had trouble with

Anne. When Fox's wife Bridget had been taken suddenly ill around five weeks prior to Torrat giving his evidence, the Vicar summoned Anne to the sick woman's bedside. Whether she went willingly or not is not known, but the purpose of the encounter was soon apparent; Bridget Fox scratched Anne hard enough to draw blood in order to break the witch's hold over her.

In consequence of Torrat's accusation, several of Torrat's neighbours made the journey to Derby to give evidence at the Quarter Sessions and statements were taken from five other Ilkeston inhabitants on 26 June.

William Smith related how, about two months before, Anne Wagg had gone to John Ellot's house to ask for milk. When this was refused she went away muttering, Smith remonstrating with Ellot that he should have provided the desired milk. The warning came too late however and the following morning, a calf that had previously been well was found dead.

The next to speak was Alice, the wife of William Day. According to her testimony, two or three years previously, she had attended a neighbour, Elizabeth Webster, on her deathbed. Webster told her friend that Anne had done her ill, though in what way Alice Day did not elaborate. Despite suggesting that it might be well to pardon Anne and thus clear her conscience before death, Webster refused and thus died with the dispute unresolved.

From Elizabeth Goddard, wife of George Goddard, the Justice was told that fifteen years previously Anne had come to her house with the request to buy some whey. Elizabeth Goddard refused the sale, telling Anne that the whey had already been set-aside for her sister. This news was not taken well and the conversation grew heated, with Anne demanding to know if her money was not as good as the other woman's. That night the Goddard's child fell ill, suffering fits and shaking for the best part of a week. Much to their relief, by the time a fortnight was gone the child was well recovered, only for Anne to visit on that very day to buy butter. Again she was sent away empty handed because there was no butter to be had, much to the detriment of the child, as it relapsed and was dead before morning.

Anne, the wife of Thomas Ancoke, had further evidence against Anne Wagg. A mere ten days before, the Ancoke's 15-year-old daughter had been taken ill and both the girl and several neighbours feared Anne Wagg was behind the sickness. At this, Anne had been summoned to the sickbed where, in front of witnesses, she and the sick girl asked forgiveness of each other.

Much to the grief of the Ancokes their daughter died not long after, but not before asserting the belief that she was 'witch-ridden', a fact she knew to be the case because at times she could not speak.[4]

The final, and perhaps most illuminating, testimony was taken from Alice, wife of William Carpenter. Not mincing her words, Mrs Carpenter asserted that Anne Wagg was of ill-repute and had been for some time. When, twelve months previously, her own child had been taken suddenly unwell, screeching and crying in great torment for a week before dying, the cause was all too clear. Calling to mind Anne's reputation, she had no trouble in labelling her neighbour a witch, certain that the evidence lay before her in the suffering and fits of her child.

What happened next is not clear. Although John Cox, in his *Three Centuries of Derbyshire Annals*, had no qualms declaring that Anne surely met a fiery fate, that is one ending that can, with certainty, be ruled out. For, as good a story as it makes, there is reliable evidence that Anne Wagg escaped the death sentence. Instead she lived out her days in the village and, according to the parish registers, was buried in the church of St Mary the Virgin in 1663, thirteen years after her neighbours saw fit to accuse her of 'being a Witch or using enchantment whereby she hath done hurt and impaired divers persons with their goods.'[5] Fiction is often considered more interesting than fact however, and the story of Anne's supposedly tortured end was repeated by Edwin Trueman in his *History of Ilkeston* at the end of the nineteenth century, enshrining the untruth and paving the way for the continuation of this misunderstanding well into the twentieth century.

Whether Anne was brought to trial and was acquitted, or whether the case did not make it as far as court is not known due to a lack of any surviving documentation other than the information taken from Francis Torrat and the other witnesses from Ilkeston at the Quarter Sessions in June 1650.[6] Gervase Bennett, the justice who took the information, must have, at least, considered the matter important enough to record the accusations against Anne in what was, effectively, a document in preparation for trial.[7] It is at this point however that Anne's case goes cold, and there is no evidence either way to confirm whether it went to trial, or was thrown out beforehand. There is the possibility that Anne might have been held in custody until the next assizes which would have been in the autumn of 1650. If this were the case, she would likely have been transferred to Nottingham Castle, or a lock up in Derby, which was without a gaol until 1652. Records for prisoners at Nottingham Castle do not exist for the period in question so it is impossible to verify this. It is possible that Anne was not held in custody, and that she may not have even come before the Justice herself.[8]

Although there is no direct mention of Anne's age in the information taken against her, a rough estimate can be made. Her husband, George Wagg, was baptised in 1604, and, allowing for the fact that she was still of childbearing age well into the 1640s, it is likely that Anne was roughly of a similar age to him. Although there is no record of their marriage, and therefore no idea of Anne's maiden name, it is likely to have occurred (if an actual marriage took place at all) around 1626 as their first child, Roger was born and, sadly, died in April 1627. Joanna and Isabell followed in the next couple of years, but did not survive their first year. The Waggs had at least eight children in total with just two, George, born 1630 and John, born 1637, surviving into adulthood.[9] An unnamed infant is recorded as being baptised in 1645 and there is the possibility that Anne gave birth to two further children in the following few years. It is likely, therefore, that Anne was between 45 and 50 at the time Francis Torratt made his accusations against her and, far from fulfilling the traditional 'old woman' stereotype, could have been as young as 30 when people first began to suspect her.

George Wagg's family is noted in the Ilkeston Manor Court Rolls from the middle of the sixteenth century with his father John, an under tenant to Thomas Eare, listed as fulfilling the requirement to attend the court on an annual basis. John Wagg died in 1621 and his wife Catherine in 1624, leaving George and his brother Roger to take over this apparently onerous duty, both being fined for absence on more than one occasion.[10] George himself was brought before the same court throughout the 1630s, charged with fighting and, the second most common offence in the area after drunken brawling, helping himself to wood that belonged to the Lord and Lady of the Manor.[11]

That there were many in Ilkeston who were not happy with Anne and her behaviour is clear from the complaints made against her. She appears to have been a woman not afraid to speak her mind; her outspoken views on the Torrats and arguments with those who refused her what she asked for are possible reasons for why she was so disliked.

Although the first rumblings go back to around 1635, the majority of the accusations against Anne refer to events that took place after George Wagg's death in 1646. It is possible that, with George's protection gone, people felt more confident to speak their minds and, not only that, to act against a woman towards whom they had long felt dislike. After all, given George Wagg's propensity for brawling and disorder (he was fined for assaulting Simon Roberts on not one, but two occasions between October 1633 and 1634 alone) it would have been rash indeed to challenge his wife without unpleasant consequences.[12] It could, on the other hand, be that Anne was at least tolerated until this point and that it was behaviour that developed around the time of George's death that led to the dislike and eventual persecution of their neighbour.

That the women of the village were reluctant to provide Anne with the commodities that were commonly shared within a community is clear in the accounts of her requests for whey and butter being refused. Although Anne is referred to as a 'beggar woman' by a later author, her case is not the familiar story of charity denied.[13] Those giving evidence made a point of the fact that Anne had the money to pay for what she required and it was they, themselves, who were either unable or unwilling to provide the goods. A combination of poor harvests, the disruption of plague in the locality a few years previously, or the lingering effects of the Civil War may have led to shortages in the area, or it may have been simply that the women were unwilling to do business with a woman of Anne's reputation.

It is in Alice Carpenter's assertion that Anne Wagg was of 'ill repute' that we find a valuable clue to unlocking the whole affair. Although missed by (or unavailable to) the Victorian reporters, the parish registers record that on 16 February 1657, a Thomas Wag, 'son of Anne, and Thomas Cant the reputed father', was buried.[14] Despite the variation in spelling, there is little doubt that this is indeed our Anne, baptising a child whose father was not her husband. There is only one other mention of the Cant surname in the registers for this period, a baptism of Henry Cant, son of Thomas, baptised 6 July 1646. George Wagg died in February 1646 and, if this child was also mothered by Anne Wagg (the register is unclear on this point, giving only the father's name on this occasion), this means she bore one, possibly two, illegitimate children as an unmarried widow.

It was possible to weather such incidents depending on your circumstances; George Wagg's brother, Roger, had a child out of wedlock with Grace, daughter of the prominent Eaton family in 1615, and salvaged the situation by marrying her a few years later.[15] John Hellot's wife, Isabell, was noted as having been the first wife of Robert Day, implying that he went on to have at least a second, while she in turn married Hellot.[16] These and other socially unacceptable behaviours such as brawling, gossiping and the fixing of prices occurred on a regular basis, but only Anne's situation was deemed worthy of open censure. Perhaps it was the manner in which the affair was carried out or the simple fact that an unmarried widow being with child was harder to ignore. There is no evidence of what happened to Thomas Cant or whether the couple lived together at any point, but that would also add further fuel to the fire.

It is also worth noting that four of the six people who gave evidence against Anne were women, who were, arguably, more likely to be intolerant of the moral transgressions of other women. The wives of William Day, George Goddard, Thomas Ancoke and William Carpenter would have had contact with Anne on an almost daily basis for a number of years as the families involved were well established in the village and in most cases had been there for as long as the Waggs.[17] If Anne's behaviour, prior to and after the death of her husband, did not fit with their ideas of what was acceptable, then that would partly explain their willingness to speak out against her. Indeed, even though it was Francis Torrat who made the initial complaint, it may well be that only after Bridget Fox, the vicar's wife, fell ill and added her voice to the rest that he felt justified in doing so, finally giving vent to the grievance harboured for three years over Anne gossiping about him and his wife.

The claims made against Anne by her neighbours reflect the common anxieties within a small community such as seventeenth century Ilkeston. Although the claim that Anne's witchcraft was responsible for the deaths attributed to her is impossible, it can be verified that those deaths did actually occur. John, son of George and Isabella Goddard, was baptised in 1635 and another son was baptised with the same name in 1639, so it is likely that the first John died as claimed in the accusations.[18] Elizabeth Webster's death, as mentioned by Alice Day, is also recorded in the parish registers and provides a good reminder that memory can be fickle. According to Alice, it was either 1647 or 1648 when she attended Elizabeth Webster on her deathbed. She was actually several years out, as the burial of Elizabeth Webster, wife of John, was recorded on 23 April 1636, putting this incident around the start of the unrest surrounding Wagg.[19] Webster was 43 at this time and her official cause of death is unknown.

Due to her reputation as a witch, several 'powers' were attributed to Anne. She was, according to her victims, able to curse through words, change her shape, and also, that well-attested power of witches, was possessed with the evil-eye – having looked at the maid and rendered her bewitched and unwell.[20] That Anne's behaviour, and the perceived results of her actions, were interpreted in such a way indicates a pre-existing belief system that encouraged people to do so. Counter, or sympathetic magic, such as the putting of the tongs in the fire also supports this. The seemingly outlandish charges against Anne would certainly not have been out of place in any of the witchcraft trials across the country throughout that century. The belief of the Torrats and their maid that Anne could turn into animal form was a staple accusation in such cases; the language used was familiar from Lord to humble baker alike. Likewise, the concept of being 'witch-ridden', as put forward by the dying Ancoke girl, would have been commonly known; the idea that a witch was, unseen, tormenting someone to the grave through malicious magic. The vicar himself shared the belief of the community, and the country at large, in witches and their power – summoning Anne so that his wife could scratch her, the well-established method of breaking a witch's power over their victim. The result of this is not recorded, but as Bridget Fox lived until at least 1657, as testified by the baptism record of a child to her in that year, it would seem that she recovered sufficiently from whatever illness Anne was supposed to have inflicted upon her.

Along with the question of why Anne was accused when many others were not, is the added question of why she escaped the death sentence so readily attributed to her case by the Victorian historians. Under the 1604 Witchcraft Act she was, after all, guilty of an offence punishable by death; causing the death of Elizabeth Webster alone would have been enough to condemn her if she had been found guilty. There are several explanations for Anne's escape from the fate that would have awaited her only a few decades earlier. The first is simply that, by 1650, witchcraft prosecutions were decidedly on the wane. The authorities were less quick to prosecute; there was a rise in acquittals, and it may be that Anne was lucky by dint of little more than timing.

Another possibility lies within the subtle politics between Church and State. Gervase Bennett, the magistrate who recorded the information against Anne, was a prominent man. He had been Mayor of Derby in 1645, and now, during the Commonwealth, was one of Oliver Cromwell's inner circle.[21] Whilst it has been lamented 'that Gervase Bennett could accept and sign such evidence leaves little doubt that his credulity on the subject of witchcraft had few limits,' it may well have been Bennett's scepticism and personal bias that saved Anne's life.[22]

Whatever his thoughts on witchcraft, it is possible that Bennett was not pre-disposed to be in favour of the deposition from Ilkeston. William Fox was instituted as vicar of Ilkeston on 4 August 1633 and he, with his wife Bridget, had at least six children baptised in Ilkeston from 1639 to 1657. Interestingly, the Report of a Parliamentary Commission of 1650, states that 'Ilkestone is a viccaridge really worth sixteene pounds per Annum. Mr Fox is minister and scandalous.'[23] Scandalous did not mean that Fox had done anything terrible, but referred instead to Royalist leanings and possibly high Anglican views, neither of which would have been to Bennett's liking.

There is also an intriguing coincidence that might have played a part. On 30 October 1650, only a few months after Anne was accused, George Fox attended a service at All Saints church in Derby where he was arrested for blasphemy and sent to the House of Correction. One of the justices who tried him was Gervase Bennett. There was no love lost between Bennett and Fox, with Fox, the founder of the Quaker movement, crediting the magistrate with the coining of the name as an insult towards him.[24] Bennett was so enraged at Fox's posturing that, according to Fox, he hit him round the head whilst he was at prayer and ordered the gaoler to take him away from his sight.[25] This still didn't stop Fox however and the unperturbed Quaker wrote a letter to tell Bennett off. It was not the first time Fox had been imprisoned and it would not be the last; it is not beyond the bounds of possibility that the particular animosity of Gervase Bennett towards him, no doubt existing for quite some time, could have led to the magistrate throwing Anne's case out through a dislike of the Fox family name.[26]

Apart from the death of her illegitimate son and her own death thirteen years later, nothing more is known of Anne after the evidence taken that June. She was, however, buried in the churchyard, something that would not likely have been allowed had she been found guilty. As it was thirteen years after the accusations were brought against her and there is no comment in the registers to say otherwise, it appears she died of natural causes. Of her eight recorded children, at least four died in early infancy, but two, George and John, lived to adulthood and married. John remained in Ilkeston with his family, being buried with his wife in 1677.[27] Despite being accused of the crimes of slander, infanticide and causing grievous harm, to name a few, Anne evidently returned to live within the community among the very same neighbours who had called her out in the first place, her family living there also for at least two more generations.

If you asked an inhabitant of Ilkeston today about Anne Wagg, you would likely be met with blank looks, perhaps a handful having a vague recollection of the story as recorded erroneously in Edwin Trueman's history. When she is remembered at all, it is as an unpleasant woman, deserving of her neighbour's dislike and, by extension, her reputed death by burning.[28] The great interest however is not that Anne died, but that she lived; surviving the process unscathed, physically at least.

Chapter Eight

Madness or Magic: Isobel Gowdie (1662)

*I was in the Downie Hills, and got meat there from
the Queen of Fairy, more than I could eat. The
Queen of Fairy is heavily clothed in white linen, and
in white and lemon clothes, etc.; and the King of
Fairy is a brave man, well favoured, and broad-faced,
etc. There were elf-bulls, routing and skirling up
and down there, and they affrighted me.*

Confession of Isobel Gowdie, 1662

Despite being united with England through the accession of King
James to the English throne in 1603, the Scottish experience of
the witch craze was very different to that of her new partner. The
witchcraft legislation passed in that year only took effect in England, and
Scotland continued to try and punish witches under the 1563 Act throughout
the Scottish 'witch hunt' that lasted from roughly 1650 to 1700.

As with England, there is some debate as to just how many were accused
of witchcraft, with the current figures suggesting the number being a little
under four thousand.[1] There have been many reasons advanced for the
greater figures in Scotland: periods of economic instability, differences in
the legal system and the existence of an organised witch-cult being but a
few. In Scotland however, it is clear that women were given much more
responsibility for their moral actions following the Scottish Reformation,
with witchcraft being part of a broader pattern of offences attributed to
women, and the final wave of witch trials in 1661–2 proving the most deadly
to date.

Isobel Gowdie, perhaps Scotland's most famous witch, was a housewife
from the small Nairnshire town of Auldearn. The reasons for her fame are
manifold, but at the centre lie the several pages that make up her confessions

which are among the most detailed and complete that exist for any witchcraft case in Britain.[2]

It is not clear from the records what prompted Isobel's arrest or even the exact date. What is known though is that her first confession was made on 13 April, 1662, before both the ministers of Auldearn and Nairn along with twelve others, made up of local lairds and elders from the church. The notary, John Inness, recorded this, and three future confessions for posterity.

In that first confession, Isobel admitted that she had met with the Devil fifteen years previously which, if her memory proved correct, meant she had been launched into the world of witchcraft around 1647. Whether she was terrified, excited, or intrigued is not made apparent, but after some discussion she agreed to meet him that very night in the kirk of Auldearn. Isobel kept her appointment, meeting the Devil in the dead of night to deny her baptism and all that came with it in the sanctuary of the church building. Her new diabolical master and associate watched from the reader's desk as she put one hand on top of her head and the other on the sole of her foot and declared, clearly and voluntarily, that she gave over all that lay between to the Devil from that moment on. They were not alone. Margaret Brodie, a woman who was to feature in several of Isobel's accounts, came forward to help them, lifting Isobel up to be baptised. The Devil scratched her shoulder, making a mark and sucking blood from the wound before spitting it into his hand and sprinkling it onto Isobel's head in a disturbing parody of the Christian baptism ceremony. When this had been done, he told Isobel that he baptised her Janet, in his name.[3] Isobel confessed that at their next meeting she had allowed the Devil to know her carnally and, although it was the first time, it was by no means the last; their coupling occurred on several different occasions during the period related.

Over the course of her confessions – taken over a six week period – Isobel was to tell of some strange and damning things that had taken place since the moment she had given herself in word and body to the Devil. She did not operate alone, but worked with a group of thirteen other witches in a 'coven' consisting of those who had also made the same pact with the Devil.[4] According to Isobel, they did much to terrorise and bring misery to those in the local area. They were also given nicknames in a way that is suggestive of some secret club or group of spies infiltrating enemy-held territory, which,

of course, is what the confessions suggest they were. These names included
the rather suggestive 'Pickle-Nearest-the-Wind' and 'Able-and-Stout'; the
dark and descriptive 'Throw-the-Cornyard' and 'Over-the-Dyke-with-It' as
well as 'Swein' and 'Red Reiver' (this is a suggestive and terrifying name
harking back to the reivers who had previously raped, pillaged and murdered
in the borders for centuries.)

One instance of their activities was an incident where she met John Taylor
and his wife, Janet Breadheid, in the Nairn Kirkyard. There they removed
from a grave the body of an un-baptised child, before taking their ill-gotten
gains some distance away to a field. Once there, they proceeded to make a
strange mixture using their toe and fingernail clippings, along with kale and
various grains. Their negative intent was proven when part of the mixture
was placed within the muckheaps of a neighbour, with the intention that his
corn harvest, and also the lambs of his sheep, would come to the members
of the coven. Another incident involved the ploughing of a field by the Devil
and the members of Isobel's coven so that the owners would receive only
thistles whilst the coven would gain the fruits of the earth. In this ceremony,
John Young took the place of the beast of burden at the head of the plough
and the Devil himself guided it through several turns around the field. All
the while the rest of the coven prayed and followed on as worshippers.

Isobel and her coven interfered not only with crops, but also with cattle
and livestock. For example, they had a special way of taking the milk from
a cow and making sure it would not produce more; a rope was plaited the
wrong way with the Devil's name called on as it was done, and then passed
between the cow's hind and forelegs in succession ensuring, claimed Isobel,
that there would be no milk from the animal until the rope was cut. Once
cut, the rope's enchantment would be broken, allowing milk to flow once
more. Apparently, the same process worked just as well with sheep. They
also conspired to ruin the local weaving economy, effectively sabotaging the
fundamentals for life, health and wealth within the local community.

Isobel also confessed that she and her coven were guilty of making attempts
on the lives of the children of the Laird of Park. John Taylor provided some
clay to a meeting of the coven; his wife had crumbled it, sieved it and watered
it whilst calling on the name of the Devil. The resultant mixture was then
shaped into a likeness of one of the Laird's sons, the face of which was laid

Tomb of Bishop Ledrede, St Canice's Cathedral, Kilkenny.

The Kyteler Slab, St Canice's Cathedral, Kilkenny.

Kyteler's Inn, Kilkenny.

Witches with their familiars.

Mill Pond, Milton Ernest. Where Mary Sutton was swum as a witch.

Title page of Witches Apprehended showing the swimming of a witch.

Indictments against Gwen ferch Ellis.

Guilty verdict against Gwen ferch
Ellis, with sentence of hanging.

Tomb inscription for Francis Manners, 6th Earl of Rutland recording his belief that witchcraft killed his sons.

Detail from Rutland tomb, showing Henry and Francis Manners, Joan Flower's supposed victims.

Witch's Cottage, Bottesford.

Matthew Hopkins and some
examples of familiars.

The Informaçon of Francis Torratt of Kedleston
in the County of Derb: Baker, taken before
Gervase Bennett Esq one of the Justices of
Peace for the County, June the Dom 1650
vpon his oath.

Concerning Ann Wagg of the same Widdow vpon suspicon of being
a witch or being inc…tant. Whereby she hath done hurt &
impaired divers persons with their goods.
Sayth she hath beene comonly suspected to bee a witch
about three yeares agone the said Ann Wagg vpon a certaine
Satterday give forth some speeches against this Infor: his wife
to Elizabeth Saxton this Infor: then serv[ant], which told this
Infor: of them & the next Lords day as this Infor: his wife
And said Eliz: Moore going to church the said Ann Wagg
stood in the way & frowned vpon the said Maide but uttered
not words & presently the Mayd fell sick & was not able to goe
a stones cast & the same night this Infor: caused the Mayd to lye
neere to this Infor: & his wife & about nine of the clock in
the night the Mayd cryed out Master W[illia]m but this Infor: &
his wife being both awake could not answer nor bring some…
… out of the Mayds bed then this Infor: gott of his bed & spake
said doe you not feele salt, looke whence that goes & this Infor: did
not stir till the salt was gone & then this Infor: went to the
Mayd & vpon that cryed out of her throate & there her voice
was stopt. And the Mayd having … heard that by putting
the tongues into the fire the woman if she was a witch would not
goe. She did put the tongues into the fire & the said Ann did
not goe till they were taken forth againe. And lately the
minister Mr Hope his wife falling suddainly sick about five
weekes since the said Ann had suspected as this Infor: sayth
heard & the said Mr Hope before her … & his wife drew
blood on her.

Ger: Bennett

St Mary's Church, Ilkeston where Anne Wagg was buried.

Witches dancing with the Devil.

A White Faced Witch and a Black Faced Witch.

A Devil and a Witch Making a Nail.

A witch at her cauldron surrounded by beasts. Etching by J. van de Velde II, 1626.

Church Yard of St Mary's, Hertingfordbury, where Jane Wenham was buried.

daily, either on a Horse, or in a Coach, I dare say it will
soon retrieve him; but if he will not, & finds himself
decay, I am very certain it will be absolutely necessary
for him to return home; before it may be too late.
where the fibres are so much relax'd, it requires
care & proper medicines to restore them; Nature can
do but little when the tone of the fibres is lessen'd.
I am very sensible of what importance his Life is
to his Family & Friends & shall be very glad, if
it lies in my power to be in any degree serviceable
to him. I perceive he has an aversion to Medicines
& therefore I must beg leave the more earnestly to
press him to a very active Life, as the surest way
to restore & secure his Health, & keep him from the
method of Cure he so much dislikes.

13. Mr Squire the Curate of Hertingfordbury gave me notice
of the Death of Jane Wenham, a poor Woman, become
famous thro' the folly of her neighbours, being the last
Woman in England (or at least in this part of it;)
that was tryd & condemn'd for Witchcraft. The Judge
who tryd her endeavourd to make the Accusation
appear ridiculous by playing on the Evidence with
a great deal of Drollery, but the Jury was so
senseless as to bring her in Guilty, & the Judge was
forced to pass Sentence of Condemnation on her to
be burn'd, however He, with my Father and Collonel
Plummer represented the Case to Queen Anne, who

by their persuasion **pardon'd Her**. I saw Jane two months
before her Death, she then retain'd a modest good look, with
a clean Complexion, & was intirely unlike what Witches
have been always represented to be; I have heard many
people say, that at the time of her Trial she was a handsome
Woman, & Jane herself always said that the Principal
Evidence against her, was a Person to whom she had
denied Favours in her youth & who always bore a spite
to her for that Reason. I am apt to believe Jane did
provoke him for she had not the sweetest of Tempers.
She had a peevish Virtue, & I suppose not only denied
the Inamorato but exposd him. My Father & Mother
always protected this poor Woman, & since their Death
our Family has continued that Protection: my Brother paid
40l. per Ann for her House Rent & the rest bestow'd their
Charity on her occasionally. About two Years ago, she fell
into a decay & made her apprehend she should die soon
& she almost starv'd her self to save something to bury
her decently, which I observing promisd to take that Charge
upon my self & on her earnest desire that her character
might be justified if possible, from yt aspersion thrown
upon it, I engaged if it cou'd be done without Risq.
that a Sermon should be preach'd something applicable
to her misfortunes. with these Promises this poor
Creature was more pleas'd than with any thing I cou'd
do to make her remains of Life Comfortable. In Consequence
of my Engagement I wrote to Mr Squire to direct the
fulfilling it & the 18th had the following Letter from
him.

Sarah Cowper's Day book describing Jane Wenham's funeral.

St Mary's Hertingfordbury pre-1891.

WITCHCRAFT
Farther Display'd.

CONTAINING

I. An Account of the *Witchcraft* practis'd by Jane Wenham of *Walkerne*, in *Hertford-shire*, since her Condemnation, upon the Bodies of Anne Thorn and Anne Street, and the deplorable Condition in which they still remain.

II. An Answer to the most general Objections against the Being and Power of Witches : With some Remarks upon the Case of Jane Wenham in particular, and on Mr. Justice Powel's Procedure therein.

To which are added,

The Tryals of Florence Newton, a famous *Irish* Witch, at the Assizes held at *Cork*, *Anno* 1661 ; as also of two Witches at the Assizes held at *Bury St. Edmonds* in *Suffolk*, *Anno* 1664, before Sir Matthew Hale, (then Lord Chief Baron of the *Exchequer*) who were found guilty and executed.

Now the Works of the Flesh are manifest, which are these, *Adultery, Fornication, Uncleanness, Lasciviousness, Idolatry,* Witchcraft, *&c.* Galat. *Chap.* V. *Verf.* 19, 20.

LONDON,

Printed for E. Curll, at the *Dial and Bible* against St. *Dunstan's* Church in *Fleet-Street*, 1712. Price 6 d. Where may be had, The Tryal and Proceedings at large against *Jane Wenham*, at *Hertford*-Assizes. Price 6 d.

Title page of *Witchcraft Farther Display'd*.

AN
Historical ESSAY
CONCERNING
WITCHCRAFT.
WITH
OBSERVATIONS upon MATTERS OF FACT; tending to clear the Texts of the Sacred Scriptures, and confute the vulgar Errors about that Point.

AND ALSO

Two SERMONS: One in Proof of the Chriftian Religion; The other concerning the Good and Evil Angels.

By FRANCIS HUTCHINSON, D. D. Chaplain in Ordinary to His Majefty, and Minifter of St. *James*'s Parifh in St. *Edmund's-Bury*.

PSALM XXXI. 6.

I have hated them that hold fuperftitious Vanities: but I truft in the Lord.

1 TIM. IV. 7.

But refufe profane and old Wives Fables, and exercife thy felf rather unto Godlinefs.

LONDON:

Printed for R. KNAPLOCK, at the *Bifhop's Head*, and D. MIDWINTER, at the *Three Crowns* in St. *Paul's* Church-yard. MDCCXVIII.

Title page of *An Historical Essay Concerning Witchcraft* by Francis Hutchinson.

Death certificate for
Susannah Sellick.

Death certificate for
Amy Gooding, one
of Susannah Sellick's
supposed victims.

Newspaper Clipping
from Western Times,
14 July, 1860.

ASSAULT.—*Virginia Ebden* was summoned by Susannah Sellick. for an assaut. The old woman is 78 years of age, and resides at Colyton Rawleigh. She went to turn her cow into a brake when defendant came up behind her. Complainant turned and said how you frightened me, to which defendant replied that she wanted to be frightened for what she "had done to she." Complainant said she hadn't "done" anything to her, when defendant scratched her face and hands, and made them bleed. Mr. Toby, on the part of the defendant, contended that the old woman assaulted the girl, and that the scratches were inflicted by brambles in the brake. The Bench disbelieved this, and fined her 5s and 9s expenses. The complainant had been looked upon as a witch, and there is little doubt this assault was committed to draw " blood," by which, according to the popular theory, the witches' power is destroyed.

Helen Duncan circa 1940.

HMS *Barham*.

Sinking of the HMS *Barham*, 1941.

301 Copnor Road, Master Temple Psychic Centre, Portsmouth.

at the fire until it 'scrunched and glowed red'. The plan was then to roast it every day, making sure that all children, both those who existed now and those who were yet to be born, would suffer. This suffering could only be stopped if the figure was broken. The figure rested, according to Isobel, in a cradle in John Taylor's house to the day of her confession.

The thing that most troubled Isobel's conscience however, were the deaths that occurred at the hands of herself and her fellow coven members. With the help of the fairies, the coven members had procured elf arrowheads; deadly objects that would kill a human.[5] Isobel and her coven would fly through the air shooting anyone they wished; the souls of their victims would go to heaven, but their bodies would remain behind as soulless husks with the coven.[6] Isobel killed her first victim (a woman) in the plough lands and went on to kill another, (gender not recorded) to the east of Murray. Bessie and Margaret Wilson, other witches in the coven, killed one person each at the same time, but these victims also remain unnamed. This was not the end of the matter; Isobel then killed a James Dick and William Bower, and it appears that this last victim, from the mill town of Boyes, was the murder that Isobel regretted most of all. She went on to detail other members of her coven who had killed in this way, eventually relating a total of fifteen incidents. The Devil also tried, successfully, to convince Isobel to shoot the Laird of Park, and Margaret Wilson to shoot the minister Harry Forbes, but both missed.

There was also the casting of malicious spells against the health of others. Isobel recounted the tale of Bessie Wilson taking a bag containing the flesh and guts of toads, mixed with nail clippings, which she swung at Thomas Reid, who promptly died, though whether due to the stench of the bag's contents or the magic supposedly created is not made clear. This was only one of the stories told about the use of magic; Isobel also confessed that the coven had used spells of this sort to attempt to take the life of Harry Forbes, the Minister who survived the attempted assassination with elf-arrows.

In the winter of 1660, Harry Forbes fell ill. Rather than offering their sympathies, Isobel and her fellow coven members took the opportunity to hasten the man's end. Given their apparent animosity toward him, their decision seems unsurprising, and their decision to do so with magic spells seems entirely in keeping with the tone of their activities so far. Accordingly and in the company of the Devil once more, the gall and guts of a toad, toe and finger nail clippings, and the liver of a hare were steeped together in water over night with the following words said, at the command of the Devil, three times over: 'he is lying in his bed and he is sick and sore, let him lie in that bed, two months and three days more.'[7] Each day the number of days would be one less, the idea being that the beleaguered minister would die when the countdown ended. Bessie Hay, being on good terms with Forbes, was charged with taking the finished bag to his house, but was unable to carry out her task of swinging the bag while he slept due to the constant flow of visitors, so their plan was foiled.

Isobel recounted how not only the Devil could change shape and appearance, (appearing in different forms each time they copulated, though maintaining cloven hooves on his feet) but also she and her friends were capable of shifting form when it suited them. She confessed how they visited houses in the form of animals and birds; Isobel herself was a kea, or jackdaw. Elspet Chisholme and Maggie Brodie were cats, while Isobel More was a hare. They changed with the following words:

I shall go into a hare, With sorrow and such and meickle [great] care; And I shall go in the Devil's name, Ay while I come home again.

And changed back with:

Hare, hare, God send thee care. I am in a hare's likeness now, But I shall be in a woman's likeness even now.[8, 9]

Another fantastical and intriguing claim made by Isobel was her telling of visits to the Downie Hills where she met none other than the Queen of the Fairies. The Queen was dressed in brown and white clothes, with white linen over the top, whilst the King, who was also present, was reputedly good looking and broad in the face. These powerful fairies were, apparently, good hosts and glad to receive Isobel, giving her more meat than she could manage to eat before she went on her way.

One of the final claims made by Isobel was that she and her fellow witches also had power over the weather and were able to raise winds. The method they used was to knock a wet rag against a stone with a 'beetle'. They would then say three times: 'I knock this rag upon this stone, to raise the wind in the Devil's name. It shall not lie until I please again.'[10] To bring the wind down again they were to dry the rag and say three times, 'we lay the wind in the devil's name ... we (or I) like to raise it again.[11] The ability to control the winds in the exposed landscapes around Inverness at this time would have been devastatingly powerful as it would have allowed Isobel and her coven to bring rain to ruin crops, cover sun to prevent ripening or manipulate weather systems to their best advantage.

Isobel's confessions were sent to Edinburgh in order to ask for permission to try her, with the expectation that she would face punishment. There does not seem to have been doubt regarding her guilt at this point and the documents suggest that a trial would be a mere formality to fix her confessions and dispense justice appropriately. Her trial most likely took place in July of that year, along with that of Janet Breadheid, whom Isobel named in her confessions. Surprisingly, not all of those indicted were gathered to face trial and no records exist to suggest why this would be so, perhaps they denied the charges or simply couldn't be found due to death or ill-health.

There is some debate regarding Isobel's eventual fate, as there is no record of the trial and therefore no firm evidence of what became of her.[12] On that basis, many say that she must have been executed; strangled and then burnt on Gallowhill outside of Nairn.[13] Others maintain that there is no reason to assume this and there is no evidence to say one way or another what happened to her.[14] One thing that is certain though, is that Isobel's name, and the fantastic nature of her confessions, have intrigued and greatly perplexed many to this day.

The information given in Isobel's rambling confessions has been hotly debated over the years.[15] The original documents were first transcribed by Robert Pitcairn in 1833, but disappeared until their rediscovery by Emma Wilby over a 150 years later. On the whole, Isobel remains a shady figure with many assumptions being passed down through the ages as 'fact'. For instance, she is generally held to have been good looking with red hair, and there has been speculation that her good looks aroused the jealousy of her fellow coven members and that this, in part, contributed to her downfall. The truth of this must remain unknown as there is nothing in her confessions, nor the records around them, to describe her appearance. She was married to a John Gibert, from Lochloy, and it is reasonable to suggest that they were tenants on the Laird of Park's estate.[16] It is also likely that this gave them a precarious economic existence, dependent on the vagaries of estate living; Isobel recounted how her husband used to sell beef to supplement their income. Agriculture would have been the main focus for Isobel's husband, consisting of the growing of grain and everything that went with it, whilst Isobel's life would have consisted of a round of domestic duties, childcare if relevant, preparation of food and production of cloth.[17]

Isobel's age is unknown, although speculation can be made in relation to the things mentioned in her confessions. She spoke of being a witch for the past fifteen years and, as the average age of marriage in Scotland in the mid-seventeenth century was 26 or 27, it is likely that Isobel was between that and 30 years of age at the time of her arrest and confessions.[18] It is not known for certain whether she had any children, but the general assumption is that she did not because they were not mentioned at any point in her confessions.

Much speculation has also been made of Isobel's mental state, with the idea that she was insane suggested as an explanation for why she confessed to such acts. To our modern way of thinking, this is a comfortable and convenient explanation, but it is by no means a given and should, in fact, be discounted for several reasons. First, there is evidence that efforts were made to ensure that Isobel and Janet Breadheid, who made her confession around the same time, were of sound mind, so dismissing their confessions as outright as fantasy is too simplistic an approach and one that ignores the subtleties and nuances of Isobel's descriptions.[19] Second, there is the argument that Isobel might have been dreaming, or in a trance, when she saw the things that she confessed to and, therefore, might genuinely have experienced the events of which she spoke.[20] Another interesting hypothesis is that what Isobel saw and experienced could be explained by ergot poisoning from eating contaminated grain such as rye or the bread that was made from it. Symptoms of this condition include mania and psychosis, and would explain the hallucinations that Isobel may have experienced.[21] However, some of the symptoms described do not fit what is known of Isobel, namely the clarity and awareness of her testimony – dullness and stupidity are listed as being symptoms of long-term consumption of contaminated rye, and Isobel's confessions suggest quite the opposite of her character.[22]

A further possible explanation is that Isobel was known as something of a storyteller within the community. Wilby, again, makes the suggestion that Isobel may have had the role of oral performer within the area, well used to story telling, and was acting within a recognised framework and pattern when she made her confessions.[23] Many elements of Isobel's confessions reflect stories that would have been shared within the village; she would have heard them during her youth on a regular basis until they were almost second nature. Whatever the trigger for her confession in the first place, their pattern, and the stories being related, were based on both her own experiences and on the oral culture of the place where she lived.[24]

Although the use of torture was common in Scottish witch trials, Isobel's case stands out in that her confessions appear to have been given voluntarily and without inducement. It must be remembered, however, that she was likely to be tired, confused and scared about what might happen to her. Sleep-deprived, hungry and alone, it is unlikely that she would have been allowed to go home throughout the gruelling six weeks covered by the dates in her confessions. She would have been vulnerable and far from comfortable; perfect conditions for the blending of lucid dreams with reality and embellishing tales of real life with fantastical elements.

For some, it is easy to find a reason for Isobel's confession. She was, quite simply, an attention seeker and an exhibitionist who combined her good memory with an even better imagination to claim her few moments of fame.[25] Isobel was, therefore, neither insane nor hallucinating, but simply enjoying her brief moment of celebrity; victim to nothing more than her own demands for attention.[26]

As in England, a 'typical' Scottish witch was female. They tended to be poor, but not markedly more than those in the community they lived in, and were generally settled rather than itinerant beggars. The crucial dynamic where accusations and prosecutions were concerned appears to have been a soured relationship with neighbours.[27] This idea is supported in Isobel's case by the fact that many of the spells performed by her coven were focused on agriculture, reflecting the malicious nature of their attacks on the major industry of the area at the time. It must also be remembered that the world in which Isobel lived, believed in witchcraft and the power it had over people. The local clergy, and those of import, were no strangers to witchcraft and the belief that they and theirs had been bewitched. Harry Forbes, had already been a victim of witchcraft by the time he arrived in the parish of Auldean as minister in 1655, and his colleague, Hugh Roso the minister of nearby Nairn, was a devout Presbyterian who had great interest in the confessions, being worried about the mortal souls of those he ministered to. Finally there was a local landowner, Alexander Brodie of Brodie, who served as judge at the trial and had previously served in other witchcraft trials of the day. He was firmly of the belief that he and his family had been targets of witchcraft in the past, making reference to the fact in his diary.

In this atmosphere of credulity and suspicion, it is not hard to imagine Isobel 'playing to type' and simply telling these men what they most wanted to hear, especially the references to attempts on the lives of the great and the good and failed efforts to kill Forbes in particular. Nevertheless, there was no evidence of personal malice toward Isobel shown; Brodie, for instance, attributed what was happening in the witch trials in Scotland as evidence that God was displeased with the behaviour of His people.[28]

Another point of contention regarding Isobel is her use of the word coven in her confessions. She makes reference to various covens in the area, and this has been taken as evidence by some to support the theory of the existence of organised groups of witches following the ideas of an ancient fertility cult. There has been much confusion over term coven throughout the years however; its simplest meaning actually refers to a meeting or gathering, not an organised group of witches and not the implication that it is often given.[29]

Isobel's confessions do illustrate that there were groups of 'witches', made up of both men and women, operating in the area, but the Survey of Scottish Witchcraft database finds no evidence of any organised witchcraft cult.[30]

Along with being the most extensive confessions existing for Scotland from a witchcraft suspect, Isobel's confessions contain the most detail regarding agreements made with the Devil. Isobel and her fellow witches gave their allegiance to their new master in a practice that was not out of the ordinary, promising everything between their head and feet to him. The Devil was not a distant figure; on the contrary, he was a very real and present figure throughout many of the events Isobel narrated and actively directed them, such as providing the elf arrows that caused so much trouble.[31]

The Devil was not only master but, if we take Isobel's words at face value, the lover of those who had given their lives to him. Whilst some enjoyed this coupling, which often took place in front of the other assembled members of the group, Isobel does not seem to have done so, complaining that he was hard and cold, and was said to be very well endowed.

Ominously, the Devil made them believe there was no god but him.[32] As a master, he demanded complete obedience, and Isobel recounted how he would beat them if they did not do as he said or spoke disrespectfully. Being absent from gatherings was also an offence punished by violence. Whilst some protested at his treatment of them, others accepted the punishments. The Devil also had the ability to change shape and he came to Isobel in her home as a crow, or deer, or another creature; this different form did not disguise him as she recognised his voice instantly.

According to Isobel, she had the great honour of being in the presence of the King and Queen of the fairies themselves, a meeting that took place at Downie Hill. Meeting with the Queen of Elphame (the name given to the Queen of the fairies in Scotland) was not uncommon in witchcraft testimonies of the time – The Survey of Scottish Witchcraft Database gives 113 results for cases that involve mention of fairies.[33] Alison Pearson was taken there on several occasions and Bessie Dunlop likewise visited. The place name 'Dunan' and its variants appears to have signified fairy hills in Scotland.[34] Examples of fairies living in hills is common in the trials and evidence of the period and it was not only the lower classes who believed such things; in 1692, the Reverend Robert Kirk wrote his famous book detailing the existence of the fairy people.[35] Isobel's description of the Queen as handsome and dressed in white linen fits with other descriptions of her and forms part of an existing fairy tradition. Like Isobel and the Devil, she was purported to be able to change shape.

It is unclear from the confessions what finally led to Isobel's arrest; it has been suggested that either the minister, Harry Forbes, or the landlord Laird of Park may have brought her to trial.[36] Any discord within the community is unrecorded, but as both featured within her confessions, it is possible, that they would have caught wind of any such untoward matters. There is also the fact that Isobel and her fellow witches targeted Forbes when he was ill, suggesting perhaps that all was not well between Forbes and his parishioners.

Isobel's case also highlights the snowballing effect of accusations and confessions. Forty-one arrests were made after Isobel and Janet Braidheid made their confessions, with no small portion of those going to the stake thereafter.

Isobel's views on her actions, whether imagined or real, seem to have left her with feelings of guilt, as she is recorded to have lamented: 'Alas, I deserve not to be sitting here, for I have done so manie evil deeds, especially killing of men etc I deserve to be reiven upon iron harrows and worse if it could be devised.'[37] From this it is fair to assume that Isobel considered herself to be guilty, at least in part, of the acts she had confessed to; that she saw herself as participating in something that could be named as witchcraft.

Isobel's memory has lived on, not only in her confessions but in the works that her words have inspired. She features in several novels, including *The Devil's Mistress* by J.W Brodie-Innes, *Isobel* by Jane Parkhurst and *Night Plague* by Graham Masterton. She has also been the inspiration behind several songs, and, musically, the most enduring contribution is James Macmillan's symphony *The Confession of Isobel Gowdie*. However Isobel has been viewed across the years, it cannot be denied that her story has touched many, and Macmillan puts voice to the feelings of many when he says:

Initially I was drawn by the dramatic and programmatic potential of this insane and terrible story but the work soon developed a far more emotional core as I attempted to draw together various strands in a single, complicated act of contrition. On behalf of the Scottish people the work craves absolution and offers Isobel Gowdie the mercy and humanity that was denied her in the last days of her life. To do this I have tried to capture the soul of Scotland in music and outer sections contain a multitude of chants, songs and litanies (real and imagined) coming together in a reflective outpouring – a prayer for the murdered woman.

This work is the Requiem that Isobel Gowdie never had.[38]

Chapter Nine

A Witch and a Bitch: Jane Wenham (1712)

If a continued course of idleness and thievery, for many years together, if the character of a whore, and the practice of common swearing and cursing will denominate a good woman we are willing to allow Jane Wenham to be one. Nay, upon second thoughts, we will allow it upon easier terms, if she can find any one in the parish that will say that he thinks her so, we will say so too.

Francis Bragge – A Full and Impartial Account (1712)

Although still technically a felony well into the eighteenth century, it was increasingly less likely to find oneself on trial for witchcraft. Often erroneously cited as the last person to be tried for witchcraft in England, Jane Wenham of Walkern can, nonetheless, lay claim to being at the centre of one of the most controversial witchcraft cases in British history.[1] Advanced in years, twice married, and with few friends and family to her name, she became well-known not only in the Hertfordshire parish in which she lived, but to names high and low across the country, even reaching the attention of Queen Anne herself.

Having lived side by side in Walkern for many years, John Chapman had long been suspicious of Jane Wenham. Cattle belonging to both him and his neighbours had died in suspicious circumstances, and he reckoned that he had lost livestock to the tune of £200 thanks to the vindictive old woman. Having no proof of the matter, he remained quiet, biding his time until at last he had reason to speak out.

How long he bit his tongue is unknown, but on 1 January, 1712, Matthew Gilston, a servant of Chapman's, met Jane while he was carrying straw for his master. The old woman asked for some of his load but was refused, at which Jane asserted that she would take some regardless. Whether she did or not is unrecorded, but on 29 January, Gilston had another encounter;

whilst threshing in the barn an old woman wearing a riding habit appeared, asking for straw just as Jane had done a few weeks previously. When he refused this second request, the woman left, muttering darkly to herself. Alone again, Gilston was seized by the sudden and irresistible desire to run. Fleeing the barn, he took off, running as far as Munder's Hill, three miles out of Walkern. No doubt exhausted, he stopped at a house where he asked for a penny worth of straw, much as the old woman had done of him. Again, mirroring the encounter with the old woman, his request was denied, and Gilston took off again towards some dung heaps. There he found the straw he was certain he needed and, successful at last, he removed his shirt and used it to carry home the coveted bundle. When questioned on his strange behaviour by others who observed him, the young man insisted that he had been compelled to act in such a fashion, although by whom or what he did not know.

Upon hearing his servant's strange tale, John Chapman became certain that Jane Wenham was behind the incident. He duly confronted the old woman and, in a heated exchange, declared that Jane was 'a witch and a bitch', making clear the animosity he felt towards this long-time neighbour.[2] What Jane said in response is not known but, on 9 February, she turned the tables on Chapman by going to Sir Henry Chauncy, the local magistrate, for a warrant against the farmer for publicly calling her a witch. On 11 February, Chauncy interviewed Jane and Chapman and, after deliberation, passed the buck by asking Jane to name someone to arbitrate in the matter between them. Jane chose the minister of Walkern, Reverend Gardiner, who listened to what both parties had to say. After his own deliberations, Gardiner's response was to make Chapman pay Jane a shilling and bid them both to try to get along better in future. Vexed by this unsatisfactory outcome at the slander against her, Jane's temper flared again as, ominously, she vowed that if Gardiner would not give her justice, she would seek other avenues to obtain what she felt was her due. The unhappy woman had good cause to regret her hasty words, as a series of coincidences ensued that were to throw her into hot water indeed.

The meeting with Gardiner took place at his home where Anne Thorn, a servant of about 16 years of age, was sitting before the fire in the kitchen. After Jane's angry exit, the Reverend, his wife, and a neighbour (a Mr Bragge who had witnessed the whole encounter) remained in the other room, only to be summoned six or seven minutes later by a terrible noise. Entering the kitchen they found Anne Thorn wearing just her shirtsleeves, speechless and distressed. Mrs Gardiner demanded an explanation for her unexpected condition. Unable to speak, the girl pointed to something that lay at her feet – a bundle that, when unpinned, was discovered to be her gown and apron wrapped around a collection of oak twigs and dead leaves.

The opening of the bundle seemed to have a curative effect on Anne Thorn and her voice returned a moment later. Still unsettled, she told her employers that she had found her mind filled with thoughts of Jane Wenham, and that, like Matthew Gilston, she had been overcome by the urge to run as far away as she could go. She had left the house, running some distance before climbing over a gate and carrying on up the hill, where she was stopped by two of Chapman's men. They tried to help her, but she was unable to accept their aid, some force keeping her away from them as she carried on in the direction of Cromer. As she reached Hackney Lane she happened to turn to look behind her, where she saw an old woman. The woman, who wore a riding hood as in Matthew Gilston's encounter, enquired where she was going. Anne replied that she was on her way to Cromer where she was to fetch sticks for a fire. The woman replied that she would not find sticks there, but instead to go to a certain oak tree that she duly pointed out to the girl. Anne obeyed and the old woman followed her. Once there, the old woman instructed her to remove her gown and apron in order to wrap her sticks up in them – Anne did so, and, lacking a pin to hold the bundle together, accepted a crooked one from the old woman, who then promptly vanished. With her dress pinned, Anne ran home with her bundle, collapsing in the kitchen where she was found by the Gardiners.

The similarity in the tales of Anne Thorn and Matthew Gilston was not lost on Mrs Gardiner, and, with a knowledge of how to deal with such matters, she quickly instructed that the sticks and pin should be thrown into the fire in order to break whatever enchantment had been cast upon their servant. In another coincidental turn of events, as the sticks lay burning, Jane Wenham herself appeared again at the door, temper now cooled and ostensibly with an errand for Anne's mother, Elizabeth, telling her that she must travel to the nearby Ardeley Bury the next day to help with the washing.

After Jane's second departure, Reverend Gardiner and Mr Bragge wasted no time in hurrying to Chapman's house, where the men who had seen Anne running were asked to confirm what they had witnessed. The men agreed, confirming what Anne had told her employers. What made the whole matter even more remarkable was the fact that Anne Thorn should not have been able to run anywhere – she had suffered an accident only the night before, putting her knee out of joint, and it had only been set in place again shortly before Jane Wenham's meeting with Reverend Gardiner.

Knee notwithstanding, the following day (12 February) the girl was well enough to be sent on an errand to a house nearby to ask Mistress Adams for some peas. Anne duly set off, only to encounter Jane on her way home. The old woman demanded to know why the girl had been making up stories about her, to which Anne boldly asserted that she had done nothing but tell the truth. At that, Jane's temper got the better of her once again, telling Anne, in no uncertain terms, that things would be worse for her if she continued to spread such tales. In the heat of the moment she pushed the servant girl, who wasted no time in telling Mrs Gardiner what had taken place when she returned home.

That same afternoon Anne fell into a terrible state once more; speechless and suffering from convulsions. She was nevertheless alert enough to make wild gestures in the direction of Jane's house, a fact taken as further sign of the old woman's involvement. Finally the girl recovered her speech and declared that she would not be well again until she had gone to gather more sticks. Despite being refused, she made several attempts to go, each time prevented by those watching her. Anne was finally permitted to go out, with Mrs Gardiner and some others following closely. To their great astonishment, Anne leapt over two five-bar gates and then kept on running until she suddenly collapsed to the ground, unable to carry on. She was picked up and the party turned back towards the house, but after going only a short way she struggled to be put down, turning back the way she had come only to fall upon reaching the same spot as before. This was repeated several times and when those with Anne tried to lead her further on, the girl screamed and shouted, saying that there was something being pressed to her throat that would kill her if they persisted.

At that, Anne was forcibly carried home, pausing to be put down to leap over each gate as she had done on her way out. Upon reaching the house she fell into a fit once more that lasted for a good while. When she had recovered a little, those with her, curious as to her behaviour, asked what had kept her from going further than the spot at which she fell. The girl's response was damning: Jane Wenham had been there and had told her that she could not fetch sticks while the others were with her, but that she could do so again when alone.

Exhausted, Anne slept off the exertions of the day, only to wake with the overwhelming urge to visit the house of the woman she blamed for her condition, declaring that she would draw blood from Jane. She did not get far before she fell into a ditch, damaging her newly healed knee once more. From where she lay she shouted to Jane who happened to be entering her house at that time, demanding that she come to her. Despite Anne and Mrs Gardiner begging her to come, Jane refused, shutting her door as the injured girl was taken home. Anne spent the remainder of the day in a state, continuing to point towards Jane's house. When the old woman was finally fetched, Anne flew at her, shouting that Jane had 'ruined' her. No doubt shaken, Jane denied having threatened the girl or being responsible for her condition, before leaving for her own home once more.[3]

Things settled somewhat the next day and Anne was sent to have her knee reset for a second time. The calm was short-lived and, arriving home around noon, she fell into another fit that was so long and violent that on more than one occasion she was thought to be dead. Eventually recovering a little, she returned to her insistence on gathering sticks, an errand that two men – Arthur Chauncy and Thomas Ireland – followed her on. The previous carry-on regarding gates and running was repeated and no matter how hard they tried to get Anne to pass through a gate, she resisted with a strength that was seen as far beyond someone of her age and size, insisting on jumping over. Once her errand was completed, she returned home again at the same pace, immediately casting the contents of her carefully collected bundle into the fire. It was only then that the girl became able to speak, relating how she had seen the old woman, who had told her that she did not need to come for sticks again before giving her a pin to pin up her bundle.

As if this strange behaviour was not enough evidence that something was gravely amiss in Walkern, in the early evening Anne grew restless once again. This time she took herself out to the river, where she tried to throw herself into the water. With great effort she was restrained and returned safely home, where she repeatedly pointed to Jane Wenham's house. It was finally decided that Jane should be fetched, but the old woman, no doubt worried by this point, locked herself in her house and would not be drawn out. Even after the arrival of the constable, who had in his hands a warrant for Jane's arrest from Henry Chauncy for suspicion of felony and witchcraft, they had to break the door down, breaking two locks in the process.

With Jane before her, Anne Thorn attacked the old woman, scratching her forehead violently with her nails. Despite the ferocity of the attack only a small amount of blood was produced, a fact that fuelled suspicions that she was a witch. Verbally attacked by her neighbours, Jane protested her innocence. Perhaps in desperation or defiance, she offered to have her body searched for teats or other known signs of witchcraft, also declaring that she would be happy to be swum. Not satisfied with this, one of the men present insisted instead that the old woman should recite the Lord's Prayer before them. Jane agreed but failed to say the prayer through without mistakes, even though she attempted it several times, damning evidence for those who already believed her to be ungodly and guilty of all manner of mischief through her witchcraft. Jane stuck each time at the lines 'Forgive us our trespasses, as we forgive those who trespass against us,' and 'lead us not into temptation', unable to say them correctly even after ten times of trying.[4]

Sir Henry Chauncy arrived in Walkern again from Ardeley-Bury the next morning, Thursday 14 February. Jane, Mr Gardiner and Matthew Gilston were all questioned on recent events and while they were giving their stories, Anne Thorn experienced another of her fits, this one so severe that those with her believed her to be dead. The young girl was taken outside, and Jane was taken to see her – whether in hope of her revival, or to reprimand the suspected witch for the suffering she had caused is unknown – when suddenly, Anne leapt to her feet, furiously attacking Jane and trying again to scratch her. Anne was forcibly removed from the scene and, instead of sympathising with the no doubt shaken and bloodied Jane, the many people who witnessed the attack saw it as yet further evidence that Anne had been bewitched by Jane. When she had recovered enough to speak, Anne in turn gave her version of events to the magistrate, her story matching those of Mr and Mrs Gardiner, and speaking most damningly of Jane Wenham and her supposed witchery.

On Chauncy's orders, Jane was eventually searched by four women, but despite their thoroughness – the search took about an hour – no marks or teats were discovered upon the old woman's body. The day had drawn on by now and Chauncy departed for home, leaving Jane in the custody of the local constable. How the night passed for Jane is unrecorded, but Anne, we are told, spent it most unhappily, falling into frequent fits from which she was only revived by the careful prayers of those attending her.

When they convened at Chauncy's house the following day, the reality of her situation suddenly hit Jane. Losing her composure she fell at Mrs Gardiner's feet and pleaded with her neighbour not to give evidence against her, as she was innocent and very afraid of what would happen if she were to be sent to gaol. She also asked again to be tried by water; Chauncy refused on the grounds that it was, by this time, illegal. Instead she was asked again to recite the Lord's Prayer by Reverend Strutt, the minister for Ardeley. As before, Jane could not get through the prayer, the same lines causing her difficulty as she stumbled over the words. Pleading confusion, Jane asked to be allowed to rest, at which Reverend Strutt said he would see her the next morning when she could again attempt to say the required prayer. Before she could rest, Jane was taken to Anne's side, the younger woman again in the grip of a fit. As before, Anne tried to attack the woman she accused of bewitching her, shouting insults at Jane until she was taken away.

Further evidence was gathered against Jane. Susan Aylott related how her sister-in-law, Sarah Harvey had believed herself bewitched by Jane before she died and how her own child had suffered and died shortly after being touched by Jane Wenham. Thomas Adam told how he had caught Jane stealing turnips from his fields a few weeks before Christmas, after which encounter he had lost a great many sheep due to their being bewitched and acting strangely, some dying from no apparent cause. Reverend Strutt returned as promised on the 16 February to give Jane another chance to say the Lord's Prayer successfully, but she could not do it; she made the same mistakes as before even though she had no trouble saying the rest of the prayer through.

Asked outright whether she had bewitched Anne Thorn, Jane equivocated. Reverend Strutt pointed out that, if she were indeed guilty, then confessing to her crimes would be the best thing she could do, both for her own soul and in order to help those whom she had tormented. With Mr Gardiner, Reverend Strutt and her relative Mr Archer as witnesses, Jane finally cracked, confessing that she was a witch, and was responsible for bewitching Anne because she had upset her at some point, though over what was not held on record. The floodgates opened. Under further probing from Reverend Strutt, Jane denied threatening Anne but that her familiar in her shape had done it instead. She also revealed that her first husband had come to a bad end and that there were rumours in the town that she had bewitched him. She said she had been a witch for sixteen years, that her 'malicious and wicked mind' and quick temper were the cause allowing the Devil to take advantage of her.[5]

Jane implicated three other women from Walkern in her confession, though it appears that these names were supplied after being asked directly, rather than volunteering the information of her own accord. Henry Chauncy sent out a warrant for the arrest of the three women, and together they were sent to Ardeley-Bury once more. Jane's supposed accomplices were duly questioned, but the magistrate found no evidence of guilt. Anne Thorn, still suffering from fits, was used as a final test. The women Jane had named were taken to her and not only spoke to Anne Thorn but touched her – with no effect. When Jane entered the room however, the girl reacted in the same violent fashion as before, once again confirming the old woman's guilt.

As matters intensified for Jane, so Anne's torments grew. She claimed to see cats visiting her, speaking to her, and appearing, she said, to resemble Jane Wenham – a fact attested to by several others. James Burvile, one of Henry Chauncy's men, and Thomas Ireland also saw the cats, which ran to Jane Wenham's house if anyone tried to approach them. Strange noises were also reported, some that sounded like cats, others that sounded more like the crying of a small child, along with scratching noises at the doors and windows that were also heard by others in the house.

It seems that Jane had made the somewhat unwise pronouncement that Anne Thorn would be well that night; a rash choice of words because her condition worsened to the point where she was believed to be stone dead, with no sign of pulse or heartbeat. As before though, the appearance of Jane Wenham (and one must feel most sorry for the old woman being so often dragged back and forth) had her on her feet once more and ready to pull the old woman apart with her own hands; this latest recovery seemed even more miraculous than those that had gone before. Mr Chauncy, one of those with her, begged Jane to remove the spell she had put on Anne, but while they were talking, a pin appeared in the old woman's hand:

> *...he knew not how, for he was very sure she plucked it out of nowhere, nor had it in her hands before, at which he snatched it from her, saying, Are you going to bewitch her again with this pin? And the maid crying out for her blood, he took Jane Wenham's arm, and ran the pin into it six or seven times, finding she never winced for it, but held her arm as still as if nothing had been done to it; and seeing no blood come, he ran it in a great many times more, still no blood came, but she stood talking, and never minded it, then again he ran it in several times more; at last he left it in her arm, that all the company might see it run up to the head.*[6]

Even this abuse did not produce the required result however as, instead of blood, all that appeared was 'a little watery serum.'[7] Far from being perturbed by her treatment, it seems that Jane spent what remained of the night (it had been rather late when she was summoned) singing and dancing, not the first time she had spent her night in such a fashion, and repeating that Anne Thorn would be well that night.

Despite Jane's assurances, Anne experienced further severe fits throughout 17 February and in addition, unexplained pins were found with startling regularity in her hands and clothing. Those with her were convinced they did not come from an earthly origin, as great care had been taken to remove all pins and sharp objects after Anne had declared that she had been tempted to kill herself. Thus started a new battle – keeping pins from Anne Thorn. However carefully they watched her, and however much they thought they had taken them all, the pins kept on coming. The baffled onlookers finally resorted to tying Anne's hands, but she still managed to get pins to her mouth, and even when her hands were tied behind her back, she still appeared to have something in her mouth that she was busy attempting to swallow.

Advice, (though from who is not stated) was taken that night to place a corked stone bottle of Anne's urine over the fire. While the bottle was heated, someone was sent to where Jane Wenham was staying to see how she responded. Jane was witnessed to be in a lot of discomfort, crying greatly, and was declared much in pain. At the moment the bottle exploded however, she was happy again; the pain disappeared and she continued singing and dancing as before.

More damning evidence against Jane came in the form of her own pincushion. Although the cushion was witnessed to be full in the evening by the two men who sat with her, by the morning, it was empty, with Jane even being in want of a pin to pin up her dress.

After spending the two days following her confession in custody, Mr Gardiner, Reverend Strutt, Mr Chauncy and Mr Bragge visited Jane at the White Horse where she was being held, and asked her to make a full confession so that it could be recorded. Perhaps with a change of heart or belatedly realising where this was leading, Jane was not as forthcoming as before, refusing this time to be held to anything that might incriminate her. When questioned about her pact with the Devil, she had no better response than that an old man had spat on her. She repeated that she had become a witch sixteen years ago and it was her mind, 'envious and wicked' that allowed the Devil his power over her.[8] She was clearly worried about what would become of her and accused those with her of wanting to take her life. Her daughter also visited and begged Jane to repent and prepare herself for death, a fact Jane did not appear to take to heart. Her daughter left, and Jane was finally conveyed to gaol in Hertford.

Even after Jane was in gaol, Anne Thorn continued to be tormented. She saw Jane herself at her window, telling her to come outside, but when Anne refused and said the Lord's Prayer, the old woman went away. Jane returned twice more but left without further incident each time. There was also the discovery of small cakes of feathers in Anne's pillow, joined together so tightly it was impossible to pull them apart. Despite Mr Bragge wanting to keep them as evidence, the Gardiners and those with them were of the opinion that they must be burnt in order to break the enchantment and so they were destroyed in the fire. The action did indeed have a positive effect, with Anne's fits stopping directly afterwards. There were still strange noises and the visitations of the cats, but these too stopped once Mr Chauncy had killed one of the creatures.

On 4 March, at about nine in the morning, Jane's trial began. Despite the many allegations made against the old woman, she was indicted only for 'conversing familiarly with the Devil in the shape of a cat.'[9] Disregarding her previous confession, she pleaded not guilty before Sir John Powell, the judge, and so the witnesses for the case were heard in turn. Anne Thorn came to give evidence first, but she suffered a fit before she could begin. Jane was brought to her, as had happened so many times before, and as usual the girl flew into a rage and tried to attack the old woman, in full view of those in the court room.

Mrs Gardiner, Reverend Gardiner and Reverend Strutt all gave their evidence, and then, as Anne was still in a fit, Reverend Chishull was allowed to pray for her. This had the much-witnessed response of Anne recovering, to the relief and gratification of at least some of those observing the event. Thereafter the rest of the witnesses gave their evidence. Mr Arthur Chauncy, Francis Bragge, Thomas Adams, Matthew Gilston, John Chapman, Susan Aylott, Elizabeth Field (Elizabeth had had a nursing child in her care who, like Susan Aylott's child, died after Jane stroked it), William Burroughs, (who had witnessed several of Anne's fits and her subsequent recovery once Jane was brought to her), Thomas Ireland and James Burvile. All related their experiences, which corroborated the story as told by Anne, each adding to the steadily growing picture of Jane the witch.

Evidence taken from the two men who accompanied Jane to Hertford was also used against her. Uriah Wright had asked Jane whether she knew the Devil and Jane had told him that she had seen him following her over her shoulder only for him to have vanished when she turned round fully to look at him. As well as this, there had been times when something came to her door and knocked three times – she knew that it was the Devil and that he wanted her to kill herself, either by hanging herself in the buttery or drowning herself in the river. Thomas Harvey, the son of Richard, confirmed what Uriah Wright said, adding that Jane had been 'reputed a witch these ten years.'[10]

After the final witness, Jane asserted that she was a 'clear woman,' denying the charges laid against her.[11] The judge summed up the evidence and the jury withdrew to consider. It was just after one in the afternoon and they deliberated until three before reaching their damning verdict.

Jane was found guilty upon the indictment of conversing with the Devil in the shape of a cat, and was duly sentenced to death.

A story that should have culminated at the gallows, however, had a very different ending thanks to the intervention of Judge Sir John Powell himself. Throughout the hearing, he made several remarks that demonstrated a decided lack of sympathy for the incredible stories he was hearing; commenting, according to one account, that it was not against the law to fly and demanding whether one witness had anything new to add to the case rather than repeating the same tired facts. Despite the verdict returned by the jury, Powell granted Jane a reprieve, allowing time for an appeal to be made for her case.

After returning home from court, Anne saw Jane at her window again and suffered from yet another fit. She was also pinched, leaving marks the size of a sixpence that eventually went black. The fits continued the next day and prayers were used to revive her each time. The pins were now absent, but instead Anne became in possession of a dagger and felt the urge to kill herself with it in her distress. Another local girl, Anne Street also spoke of being bewitched by Jane Wenham. A 'very brisk, healthful maid' she had started to suffer from fits much in the same manner as Anne Thorn, starting on 17 February.[12] She likewise felt the urge to drown herself, needing three men to drag her from the water, or choking herself with the sheets from her bed, even though she was watched closely. Prayers helped and, as with Anne Thorn, Anne Street's thoughts were much taken with Jane Wenham.

In the meantime, everyone had an opinion on Jane. For every person who declared her a witch, there was another who thought the contrary; the debate raged far and wide. Finally, much to the great satisfaction of her supporters, Jane was granted a pardon and the charges against her dropped. Colonel Plummer of Gilston in Hertfordshire took up Jane's case and, not considering it prudent for her to return to Walkern, he took her to live in a house on his own estate where, in 1718, she was recorded as living 'soberly and inoffensively.' Francis Hutchinson, the author of the 1718 pamphlet *An Historical Essay Concerning Witchcraft* says he saw Jane Wenham in person, vouching for her as a 'pious sober woman,' perfectly capable of saying the Lord's Prayer.[13]

Plummer died in 1720, and Jane lived out the last decade of her life on the estate of Lord Cowper, dying in 1729 at close to 90 years old and outliving the major players in the case against her. Jane died in mid-December 1729 and was buried in the churchyard at St Mary's, Hertingfordbury. Rev Mr Squire, curate of Hertingfordbury read the sermon at her funeral, which was paid for by Lord Cowper's daughter, Lady Sarah Cowper and was well attended.[14]

That Jane survived her guilty verdict was a sign of the times in general. Although belief in witchcraft amongst the lower orders was still common, the willingness of the authorities to act against accusations was waning. Indeed, it was somewhat surprising that the case against Jane got as far as it did, perhaps as a result of the vociferous nature of those who spoke against her. There were no less than nine pamphlets written about the case, with opinions both for and against Jane. Her main detractor was Francis Bragge who, convinced of her guilt, poured out more words against her than anyone else.[15]

The fractious nature of Jane's relationships within the town of Walkern is clear from the evidence given against her. Amongst others, Susan Aylott told how, some dozen years previously, she had been summoned to attend Sarah Harvey, the wife of her brother Richard Harvey, who was suffering from a 'strange condition'.[16] Having been previously informed by Sarah Harvey that Jane had bewitched her, Susan Aylott had been surprised to find Jane herself following her on her visit. Not entering the house, Jane instead had contented herself with standing beneath the window, shouting insults about the sick woman. Susan Aylott had told her to go away, whereupon Jane told her to hold her tongue, as it was not she with whom she had the quarrel. Mrs Harvey passed away that night.

Another incident that stuck in Mrs Aylott's mind took place not long after. Perhaps seeking to make amends, Jane visited the Aylott household, remarking that the child there was 'curious', and stroking it with her hand.[17] Acknowledging that they had 'had some words' in the past, Jane expressed the hope that they could be friends after all, before asking for a glass to fetch some vinegar from the shop.[18] Susan Aylott duly loaned this to Jane, and the old woman departed, but Susan remembered feeling very afraid for her child as she recalled what had happened to her sister-in-law. She was right, it seemed, to be fearful; whilst visiting her brother Jeremy Harvey the following Sunday, her child was taken ill and died four days later. Susan was thereafter convinced that not only was Jane Wenham's reputation as a witch justified, but that she had been responsible for the death of her child.

More damningly for Jane, there was good reason for her to wish those related to the Harvey family harm. At some point in the past, Edward Wenham, Jane's apparently absent husband, had asked Richard Harvey to have the town crier publicly announce that he, Wenham, renounced his wife and would not be responsible for her debts or well-being. Richard Harvey had agreed and carried out Edward Wenham's request, thereby providing a perfect motive for Jane to harbour animosity against the Harvey family, including Susan Aylott.[19]

Pleading poverty, Anne Street and her friends and family did not attend court themselves. They did, however, live in hope that the witch that tormented the girl would be brought to justice. This was common and it often took action from someone higher up the social hierarchy with the money and connections to start a case; only then did others come forward to report grievances that had been going on for years. For most however, the journey times, bad state of roads and the expense of both travel and bringing action against a suspected witch, meant that there was little choice but to keep their grumblings to themselves.

Interestingly, Jane's own admission to being a witch for sixteen years goes back to 1696, the year that her first husband, Philip Cooke, died. He was buried in the parish church of St Mary in November of that year.[20] Jane's subsequent marriage to Edward Wenham came very quickly, taking place in February 1697, which set local tongues wagging, and, by the time of her arrest, had become whispers that she had been instrumental in Cooke's death.[21]

It was declared that even Jane's own family rejected her and believed her guilty of the crimes laid against her. A relative by the name of Archer from Sandon washed his hands of Jane after witnessing her inability to say the Lord's Prayer on the final attempt with Reverend Strutt on 16 February, and her confession to bewitching Anne Thorn. Jane had at least two children with her first husband and there are two children recorded born to Philip and Jane Cooke in the parish registers for Walkern. Elizabeth Cooke was baptised there on 6 December, 1679, while Sarah Cooke was baptised on 18 December 1681.[22] Sarah at least visited her mother, but after her pleading with Jane to confess for her own good fell on deaf ears, she left and there is no further mention of Jane's children.[23] Edward Wenham is not recorded as having visited, or spoken for or against, his wife at any point and is conspicuous only by his absence during the entire case against Jane.

Alone, friendless, and isolated, it is perhaps not as surprising as it first seems that Jane admitted to the accusations against her. It has been posited that those in economic or social disstress would confess with the actual intention of being destroyed, in essence committing suicide.[24] In this process, the confession acted as a plea for forgiveness and the hope of reintegration within the community.[25] Certainly, one can see this in Jane's references to feeling that the Devil wanted her to kill herself by hanging or drowning. This suggestion was shared by the author of one of the pamphlets produced on Jane's case; sympathetic to Jane and refuting one by one Bragge's arguments against her, the author opined that:

> *Methinks a poor woman, that has lived for sixteen years under the character of a witch, and by this means was become so odious to all her neighbours, as to be denied in all probability, the common necessaries of life, should have enough upon her to make her sick of the world, and desirous of being removed out of the reach of these misfortunes.*[26]

Jane's assertion that three other women were guilty of witchcraft in Walkern at the time is deeply intriguing, but unfortunately there is nothing to indicate who these women might have been and, although Jane named names, they were not recorded in any of the surviving sources and are now lost to us. Along with her already bad reputation in the town, there was talk that Jane stood out in more ways than one. Jane was of the opinion that she had been targeted not for her witchcraft, but for her attendance at local dissenter meetings, and it was alleged that she received both money and support from that quarter.[27]

What of Anne Thorn, Jane's supposed victim? In Bragge's first account, the reader is informed that Mrs Gardiner vouched most sincerely for the good character of her maid, praising her for her 'Sobriety, Diligence, and good Temper, by which she had gained the Love of all the Neighbourhood.'[28] The sorrow she felt at Anne's condition was, it seemed, so great, that she took her children and moved into a neighbour's house as she was so tired and worn down with grief at the whole situation. This incident is regarded in a different light however by the author of *The Case of the Hertfordshire Witchcraft Consider'd*, one of several pamphlets written in response to Bragge's account. The author claims to have spoken to many involved in the case, and that, far from upholding her former opinion of Anne, Mrs Gardiner now had 'so much reason to alter her opinion, that … she will not now say any thing in her defence.'[29] Indeed, whatever Anne Thorn's reputation beforehand, 'She is at last found to be so *arrant a liar*, that there is no manner of heed to be given to any thing that she says.'[30]

The interesting turn of phrase used by Anne Thorn against Jane Wenham several times was that the older woman had 'ruined' her. This Wenham vociferously denied, but what did the younger woman mean by it? One possibility is that Anne Thorn may have been pregnant and gone to Wenham for help in dealing with the situation. When Jane either refused, or was unsuccessful in her endeavours, it is possible that the young woman, fearful of how she would be treated if her secret was discovered, not only worried herself into the terrible state related, but also saw Jane Wenham as being to blame for her condition and downfall in the first place. Or perhaps she had gone to Jane for a love spell, and it had worked only too well, the results not what Anne Thorn, a girl of 16 or 17 years of age, had anticipated. As it was, all turned out for the best. At the suggestion of a white witch consulted in the hope of affecting a cure, Anne Thorn washed her hands and face daily in the water given to her and was attended by a 'young, lusty man'. The result was exactly as predicted. We are told that:

The man who attended her by the doctor's order is now become her husband, which had so good an effect upon her, that notwithstanding all her former illness, she was able within a day or two to follow her Bridegroom into Wales (as some say) or some other place a great way of [sic] it is not well known where.[31]

An entry for 27 April in the Hitchin Marriage Registers records the marriage of 'James Bonnill or Bonvill of Maldin in the County of Bedford and Anne Thorn of Walcon [sic] in the county of Hertford.'[32] If they did indeed move to Wales or 'some other place a great way off'' it might be wondered what prompted this sudden move. Without knowing where to look (and a cursory look at the registers available for Wales for the relevant time reveals nothing pertinent under the surname) the whereabouts of Anne Thorn and her new husband remains, for now, a mystery.[33]

There is a final mystery where Jane is concerned. Although reference is made to her burial in Hertingfordbury Churchyard in the daybook of Sarah Cowper, daughter of William, 1st Earl Cowper, who paid for her funeral, there is no record of Jane's burial in the Hertingfordbury Parish Registers. A search of records for other parishes nearby and Jane's native Walkern also shows no sign of a burial record for her. It is therefore to be assumed that she was indeed buried at Hertingfordbury, but that it was not recorded, her grave unmarked in order to deter vandalism. Thus Jane remained a source of controversy even after her death, and to this day people continue to hold strong views regarding the Witch of Walkern.

The story of Jane Wenham has been recreated in both novels and for the stage. The most recent adaptation of Jane's story was the gripping and gritty 2015 play *Jane Wenham: The Witch of Walkern* by accomplished playwright Rebecca Lenkiewicz and Out of Joint Theatre. By turns amusing, chilling and poignantly thought provoking, this captivating piece of theatre transcends the historical record to present a relevant, modern, frequently uncomfortable but entirely necessary take on witch hunts, both then and now. It could be argued that Jane's story is one that will never grow old, and it is fitting and right indeed that she will never be forgotten.[34]

Chapter Ten

A Victorian Witch: Susannah Sellick (1852–1860)

The time is come, nevertheless, when we have ceased to become the fulfillers
of a declaration by chaining to a stake and roasting alive every miserable
old woman whose toothless gums and wrinkled visage marked her out as
an accursed being, sold to the evil one to do his bidding, in executing his
malicious designs on others.

Somerset County Gazette, 13 August, 1864

The year 1736 saw a victory of order over chaos, enlightenment over superstition, common-sense over the irrational. For in June of that year, an Act came into effect that removed forever the legal possibility of witchcraft.[1] The time was ripe for such legislation and the actual passing of the Act saw little opposition with those involved in the process pleased that the era of superstitious belief was at an end.

Although the writer of the Somerset Gazette quoted above was right that the legal persecution of witches was over, his optimism was somewhat premature where the general populace was concerned. Belief in the existence of witches and the very real danger they posed to health and happiness did not vanish overnight, and it was not an easy duty for those in positions of authority on a local level such as the clergy and magistrates to enforce the Act and make sure that people knew of, and abided by, the changes therein.

This was nowhere more in evidence than in the West Country areas of Somerset, Devon and Cornwall, with reports of attacks on suspected witches continuing well into the nineteenth century. One thing had most certainly changed, however; those accused of witchcraft were no longer helpless victims at the mercy of those who called them out. On the contrary, the new Act meant that those who were harassed and attacked due to suspicion of witchcraft were now able to seek protection and justice. That many did so is clear from the remaining records of the time; with many an accused witch triumphant as her attackers looked on in bewilderment that the authorities were no longer on their side and often found themselves facing a fine or imprisonment for their troubles.

It was in just such a situation that Susannah Sellick of Colaton Raleigh, Devon, brought a case to court in 1852 to seek justice against her neighbours. Born just shy of fifty years after the passing of the act that made the belief in witchcraft itself illegal, Susannah took advantage of this protection that had not been available to her predecessors, bringing those who tormented her before the courts.[2] The first mention of Susannah's troubles occurred in the *Exeter and Plymouth Gazette* for 24 April 1852, where it was reported that the 70-year-old woman had brought action against Mary Pile and Walter Gooding at the Woodbury Petty Sessions for assaulting her. According to the report, Susannah had encountered the two when she was out walking and, as they drew nearer, Mary Pile called out: 'Why have you hurted my daughter?'[3]

Without giving Susannah a chance to reply, the woman then attacked her, scratching her face badly in the process. Walter Gooding, meanwhile, far from coming to Susannah's aid, was busy attempting to assist his accomplice by kneeling on the ground with his hands under Susannah's skirts and doing his best to drive a nail into the ground beneath her feet.

During the unprovoked attack, William Shute, a neighbour, happened upon the group. Perhaps sensing he would not be sympathetic to their cause, Mary Pile and Walter Gooding made themselves scarce, leaving him to help the badly shaken Susannah.

When questioned by the court, Mary Pile, aged 45, insisted that she was fully justified in attacking Susannah, as drawing blood was essential. It seemed that Mary was convinced that Susannah had bewitched her daughter and that she had gone to 'fetch her blood' in order to break the spell.[4] She claimed it had taken five men to hold her daughter down before the incident with Sellick but, as soon as she had drawn blood from the old woman, her daughter had been herself again, thereby proving Susannah guilty of witchcraft. Walter Gooding was also deeply convinced of the truth of this, maintaining that he had only done what was necessary to help the suffering young woman, who turned out to be his wife. He was certain that hammering a nail into the ground below Susannah's feet would likewise break the enchantment and the power that the old woman held over his spouse.

Also in the courtroom to give an account of what she had been through at the hands of Susannah was 20-year-old Amy Gooding. The young woman claimed that Susannah had often been in her house over the past two years – though whether by invitation or not was not made clear – and that these visits corresponded with her own troublesome periods of illness. Matters had come to a head a fortnight prior to the court case with a strange occurrence that could not be ignored. Amy had been wearing a string around her neck but, upon retiring to bed, found that it had disappeared. As midnight drew near a loud knock had sounded at the door, followed by a second, this time at the foot of Amy's bed. A final knock sounded against the bed itself and, terrified, the young woman found she could not move, an unexplained and unseen heavy weight against her chest keeping her pinned down.

Whether she had fallen asleep naturally, or passed out from fright, the string was once more safely around Amy's neck when she woke in the morning. This was little comfort, however, as from this point on Amy insisted that Susannah had been 'continually with her'.[5] Her evidence for this was several signs; the most compelling, according to Amy, being that it was impossible to keep a candle burning in the house as the witch insisted on extinguishing them. Not only did her husband's candle keep going out, but it even moved location – discovered one morning downstairs in the clothes basket. All of this served as proof of Susannah's powers of witchcraft and her deployment of them against the family and Amy in particular.

Susannah's rescuer, William Shute, was then called to give his version of events, describing Susannah's bloodied state and the old woman's distress at the unprovoked attack. He did not comment on the claims that the old woman had done harm to Amy Gooding and there is no evidence that the court sought any further witnesses to verify the claims made to justify the attack. When Susannah was called to the stand she was adamant that, not only had she done Amy Gooding no harm, she did not even know the woman in question.

The magistrates did their best to reason with Mary Pile, Walter Gooding and his wife, explaining in no uncertain terms that what they were maintaining was little short of ridiculous. Their attempts were in vain however, with the defendants clinging to the belief that Susannah Sellick's witchcraft was at the root of Amy's suffering and that the old woman needed to be dealt with. Faced with such unconquerable certainty, the magistrates finally resigned themselves to the futility of the attempt, suggesting instead that perhaps they might do well to visit the local clergyman to find what he had to say on the matter, no doubt hoping that he would be able to talk sense into the group where they themselves had failed.

They did have some power to enact justice and Mary Pile was fined £1 13s, whilst Walter Gooding was fined £1 3s, both including costs.[6] The Magistrates went on to inform Susannah that if she had further trouble she should not hesitate to return to them, adding with little concealed weariness that this was the third case in the area within as many months of assault on old women suspected of witchcraft.

Unfortunately for Susannah, the incident was not the end of her troubles, and in 1860 she had cause to come before the courts again for assistance. She attended the Woodbury Petty Sessions on Monday 9 July of that year, with the complaint that Virginia Ebdon, an 18-year-old lace-maker, had maliciously assaulted her on 8 June. According to Susannah, she had been tending her cow when the young woman appeared. During the encounter the following exchange took place:

Susannah: "How you frightened me!"
Ebdon: "You wanted to be frightened for what you ha' done to me."
Susannah: "I have'nt a doo'd nothing to you."[7]

Virginia Ebdon then attacked Susannah, now aged 78 years old, scratching her face and hands hard enough to draw blood. This was indeed the girl's intention, as it had been Mary Pile's eight years previously. As she gave her story, Susannah revealed that at the time she had been deeply afraid, certain that Ebdon had meant to kill her. She also appealed to a Mr Holmes who was present both at the court and during the incident itself, asking him, 'You saw it, Sir, bleeding.' regarding her wounds.[8] As with the earlier attack, Susannah was adamant that she did not know why she had been scratched and attacked whilst going about her own business, certain that there had been no just cause for Virginia Ebdon's actions.

Mr Toby, acting on behalf of Virginia Ebdon, gave quite another version of events. According to this story, the young woman had been watching a donkey belonging to her grandfather when Susannah approached her and called her names before chasing her with a stick, frightening the young woman badly. Fearful for her safety, Virginia had run to where her grandfather, John Ebdon, waited, seeking refuge with him.

John Ebdon also gave his story. Interestingly, he did not seem to come down on the side of either party, saying only that he had witnessed the older woman running after the younger with a stick and that he thought his grand daughter had hold of the other end of it. He did not comment on any distress from either party, maintaining that neither woman had made any complaint to him as they approached.

Susannah denied holding a stick over the younger woman or running after her, although she admitted to having a small umbrella stick with her that she used to drive her cow. She also pointed out, however, that she could hardly have been expected to remain where she was indefinitely and it might be inferred from this that she did indeed try to defend herself, either physically or verbally, from Virginia Ebdon's attack.

After hearing all the evidence, the court again declared for Susannah, with Virginia Ebdon fined 14s to cover costs. The newspaper account ends with a lamentation that belief in witchcraft was prevalent amongst the illiterate in the "'eighborough' of Colyton, Salterton and Woodbury.[9]

Colaton Raleigh of the mid-nineteenth century was not a good example of the reason and sense that the new legislation had sought to create. At the time of the incidents involving Susannah, it was described as a 'Straggling Village' of 3,331 acres of land, with 840 inhabitants.[10] Susannah had been born there in 1783 to John and Elizabeth Bolt and was baptised in the church of St John the Baptist on 8 March.[11] She was one of eight recorded children of the couple, and was either the eldest or second eldest. The record is silent on her early years, but she married Henry Sellick on 28 December, 1808, at the age of twenty four.[12]

How Susannah's reputation as a witch began is unknown. As with earlier cases, it is clear that tensions had been brewing long before Mary Pile and Walter Gooding decided to act on their belief that the old woman was responsible for the suffering of young Amy. It is also likely that they were not the only ones to believe Susannah guilty of witchcraft because the backing, or at least tacit support, of others within the community of Colaton Raleigh would have been a necessary spur to carry out the attack. She was not shunned by everyone however, because William Shute had come to her aid, so it is entirely possible that opinion was divided within Colaton Raleigh on Susannah's reputation as a witch.

By 1841 Henry and Susannah were living in Lower Hawkerland, Colaton Raleigh and Henry Sellick is listed as an agricultural labourer.[13] In 1851, the year before the incident with Mary Pile and Walter Gooding, Henry and Susannah were in Lower Hawkerland House, with Henry farming five acres of land, not insubstantial property for the couple.

There is some discrepancy regarding Susannah's marital status in 1852 –the newspaper reports refer to her as a widow, but the only death record present for a Henry Sellick is from 1860, which states he died at the age of 74 and was buried at Colaton Raleigh.[14] The death certificate for the individual in question confirms that this Henry Sellick and Susannah's husband were one and the same, his death occurring on 18 October 1860; not only well after the attack on Susannah by Mary Pile and Walter Gooding, but also three months after the altercation with Virginia Ebdon.[15] What Henry Sellick made of the attacks on his wife can only be guessed at because of there being no record of his presence or opinion at either of the court cases attended by his wife.

Susannah and Henry Sellick do not seem to have been living in reduced circumstances and, in the 1860 account, Susannah was described not only as respectably dressed, but healthy-looking. There is also no evidence that she was guilty of the old common complaints of begging or otherwise bothering her neighbours that so often accompanied accusations of witchcraft, a reflection of the reduction in such cases into the nineteenth century.

Whilst the existence of 'white witches' and of cunning men and women was widespread in the West Country during this time, there is no evidence to suggest that Susannah provided this role within her community. It is more likely, in fact, that such a practitioner – renowned for detecting the whereabouts of stolen goods, performing love magic, or producing charms and potions for a number of ailments – would have been responsible for pointing the finger at Susannah in the first place, confirming existing suspicions.

Although both the Sellicks and Bolts were prolific when it came to reproducing, it appears that Henry and Susannah had only one child: Caroline Sellick. Caroline was baptised on Christmas Day, 1813, but died in 1816 at the age of four.[16] The couple do not appear to have had any further children. This did not leave Susannah without family however, as several branches of both Sellick and Bolt families are listed as present in the village during the period in question. After the death of her husband, it seems Susannah was living with Caroline Bolt. Caroline was related by marriage (she married Susannah's cousin William and may also have been a cousin of Susannah's in her own right.) Caroline was also widowed and her own daughter, Sarah, was living with the two older women.[17]

As with the incidents involving Susannah, most cases reached the courts after the suspected witch had been attacked by her accusers, most often in an attempt to draw blood from her.[18] It is clear from the attitude of the magistrates that these accusations were not uncommon especially in their advice to Susannah that she should return if there was further trouble; there was also mention of three similar incidents within as many months.[19]

In both cases, the attacks against Susannah were prompted by the desire to break the perceived bewitchment the attackers felt she held over them or their loved one. In both cases, the primary aim seems to have been the drawing of blood in the belief that this would relieve the victim – one of the most enduring beliefs over the centuries. William Shute's description of Susannah's bloodied and shaken state gives a clear indication that the drawing of blood was a far more violent act than a simple, symbolic scratch.[20]

The driving of a nail into the ground was also significant in the matter of the counter-magic in which Mary Pile and Walter Gooding were employed. Iron, and nails in particular, had long been associated with protection and cures.[21] There was a belief that a witch could be detected by driving an iron nail into her footprint – if guilty as suspected, the woman would feel a burning sensation in her foot and be drawn to the place to remove the nail. She would feel nothing if not a witch.[22] An intriguing artefact held by the Museum of Witchcraft in Boscastle, Cornwall is particularly worthy of note: a large iron nail with a slip of paper states that an old country remedy for epilepsy was driving a nail into the ground where the victim fell. This is of particular relevance to Susannah's case as it was reported that Amy Gooding was suffering from epileptic fits at the time of the attack on Susannah.

Incidentally, this is not the only time a member of the Bolt family was involved in a witchcraft case. According to the *Exeter and Plymouth Gazette* on 6 October, 1860, John Bolt of Aylsebeare was charged with assaulting his mother, Mary Bolt, with a shovel. She had taken him to task over the neglect of his children when he had lost his temper, hitting her twice on the back with the shovel he was using in a gravel pit. He declared that he had known her to be a witch for the last two years, and that if his horse was to fall down dead, it would be her bewitchment that caused it. He was found guilty and paid a fine of £3 in order to avoid a period of imprisonment. Mary and John Bolt were probably related to Caroline Bolt, who had married Susannah's cousin William and with whom she ended up living out her days, both coming from the Aylesbeare branch of the family.[23]

The variety of sources available when examining witchcraft cases increase with the nineteenth century. The court to which Susannah sought redress was the local petty sessions for Woodbury. Survival of records for Petty Sessions for the time are generally low however, and none survive for Woodbury from the time of Susannah's cases.[24] The best sources for what occurred in the courtroom are actually the newspapers of the time, providing a rich seam of detail regarding the cases that went to court. Accounts of what was actually said, the appearance of those in attendance, and the reaction of those watching were all recorded to a greater or lesser extent, details that were generally lacking from standard court records.[25]

Interestingly, the tone of two reports of the incident with Virginia Ebdon in 1860 differ from each other. According to the account in the *Taunton Courier and Western Advertiser* there was 'some tradition' involving drawing blood from a witch, but the report was at pains to stress that there was no sign that this belief had anything to do with the case in question.[26] This is directly contradicted by the telling in the *Western Times* supplement, which states that Susannah had long been seen as a witch, and that there was 'little doubt' that the attack had been committed with the intention of breaking the power of the witch over her supposed victim.[27] This highlights the conflict that still existed between belief in witchcraft on a local level and the wish of those in authority to distance themselves from it.[28] In none of the reports does it state what Susannah was actually supposed to have done to Virginia Ebdon, though it must be assumed that bad blood had existed between them prior to this point, due to the younger woman's insistence that Susannah deserved to be scared for what she alleged had been done to her.

The church of St John the Baptist at Colaton Raleigh, scene of some of the major events in Susannah's life and where she found her final resting place, was also the repository for the records of baptisms, marriages and burials for the village. These records offer a selection of information and insights into village life as far back as 1673.[29] In addition, with the advent of the 1836 *Births and Deaths Registration Act*, every birth, marriage and death in England had to be recorded.[30] By far the most useful source of information after newspapers however, was the beginning of the census records. Starting in 1841, a ten-yearly census was taken recording the whereabouts of every individual in England, Wales and Scotland on a designated night.[31]

From a combination of these sources, it is clear that the families of Colaton Raleigh were closely intertwined and the community close-knit. The same families are present consistently throughout the records, with members of the Bolt family acting as witnesses to several Sellick marriages, with intermarriage between both families and, interestingly, with the Goodings and the Piles.

Through these sources, a picture can also be pieced together of those who assaulted Susannah. At the time of the first assault, Amy and Walter Gooding had been married for three years. The 1851 census shows the couple living in East Budleigh, where Walter is listed as a labourer and Amy herself as a dress-maker. There is also record of a child, 10-month-old Adam Gooding. Amy was born in 1830, making her just over 20 years of age at the time her mother and husband attacked Susannah on her behalf.

It appears to have been an unsettled time for the Gooding/Pile families in a number of ways; as well as having a young child and Amy's illness to contend with, there was also the possible illness and eventual death of Robert Pile, Mary Pile's husband.[32] There is little doubt that the family felt lacking in a certain amount of control over what was happening to them, and the allegations against Susannah, read in this context, could be seen as an attempt to exert some personal control over their conditions.

For Walter and Amy Gooding the brush with the law, or possibly the unshaken belief that the elderly Susannah was responsible for their suffering, may have proved too much. They left the area not long afterwards, their course traceable through the census records. By 1861 the couple were in Durham, Walter working as an iron heater at the iron works there. Their daughter, Anne, had been born in 1854 in Wales, meaning that they must have left the Colaton Raleigh area by that year at the latest. Whatever fears there were for Susannah's hold over Amy appear to have been unfounded: she outlived her husband by several years and, in 1881, was recorded as living in the family home in Durham with her children. She remained there until her own death from heart disease aged 68 and was buried on 27 May in Oxbridge Cemetery. Mary Pile, on the other hand, remained in Colaton Raleigh after Amy and Walter left, living with a lodger at the time of the 1871 census and dying at the age of 81 in 1886. Did she remain convinced that Susannah was a witch to the end of her life? It might have been rumours and talk of the previous incident that led to the attack by Virginia Ebdon several years later.

Of those involved in the second assault, Virginia Alford Ebdon was baptised in Colaton Raleigh in 1842, recorded as the natural daughter of Elizabeth Ebdon. Elizabeth's parents were John and Elizabeth Ebdon, John being the grandfather involved in the story. In 1851, Virginia is listed as living with her grandparents and a lacemaker. In 1861, not long after the incident, the younger woman was living with her widowed Grandfather, John Ebdon, and was listed as 18 years of age. By 1881 she was living with the Vinnicome family and listed as married but, interestingly, retained her maiden surname. This, coupled with the lack of a marriage record, suggests that no marriage had actually taken place, despite having a daughter named Elizabeth born in 1872, listed in baptism records as Elizabeth Alice Ebdon.[33]

The Reverend Noel Lowe, vicar of St John the Baptist until 1857, would have been the member of clergy that Mary Pile and Walter Gooding were directed to by local magistrates for instruction in the error of their ways. It is not clear whether accusations about Susannah were ever made to the vicar or local magistrates, because both times offences were reported, Susannah herself had brought them to court. It may be that Walter Gooding and Mary Pile took it upon themselves to try to break Susannah's power precisely because the vicar had refused to listen to them in the first place, as those in authority sought to distance themselves from such things after the passing of the 1736 Act. Whatever the personal beliefs of the Reverend Lowe, whatever he might have told Pile and Gooding, was not enough to stop the gossip that led to the second attack on Susannah in 1860, and he would have been limited in what he could do to help the old woman. Frederick Bullock, vicar from 1857 until 1903, would have been similarly unsympathetic to complaints of witchcraft.

In the end, it is clear that the nineteenth century saw its fair share of accused witches, with local and rural communities remaining just as convinced as ever that their ills had a supernatural cause. The prevalence of 'old wives' tales' and the longevity of folk remedies in medicine, coupled with the insular nature of these societies, made such beliefs easy to maintain despite the creation of a more 'rational' set of beliefs dominating in the towns and cities. Despite the advent of trains, technology and the triumph of the Industrial Revolution, it is clear just how tenacious the belief in, and fear of, witchcraft was in these supposedly enlightened times. Although the names of those accused and assaulted, as they had been for so long, are generally unknown, to be accused was not yet a thing of the past and cases continued to be brought long after the passing of the Act designed to limit the official recognition of the supernatural in everyday life.

As for Susannah, whether she faced any further accusations of witchcraft during her lifetime or not is unknown, the newspapers that recorded her two court appearances remaining steadfastly silent on the matter. She was buried at the age of 96 on 23 March, 1879 at the church of St John the Baptist, Colaton Raleigh, finding, it must be hoped, the peace that had for so much of her life eluded her.[34]

Chapter Eleven

The Conspiracy of the Last Witch: Helen Duncan (1944)

If that be true, that was heard by other people present. It was heard, members of the jury; the voice was heard, and the features of the child were seen. I beg of you, look always throughout my evidence for features plainly seen a nose, a mouth, ears because you may very well be thinking that that cannot be done by Mrs. Duncan playing bogey-bogey with a sheet over her head—eyes, nose, mouth, ears, birthmarks, and that kind of thing. I beg of you to be looking for that kind of thing.

The Trial of Mrs Duncan, C.E Bechhofer Roberts.

There are few questions that have more consistently taxed humankind over the centuries than that of what happens after death. Although explanations and theories have changed across time, the central need for understanding and reassurance have remained constant; with each new generation adding to or rejecting the beliefs that have come before. What happens when we die, and the desire to believe that something does carry on after we do, are constant vexations throughout recorded history.

This preoccupation with death seems to come to the fore during times of high mortality and uncertainty: wars, plagues and famines. Britain in the early twentieth century experienced one of the greatest periods of loss and grief known in the country's history, the First World War, when an estimated 711,000 British servicemen lost their lives.[1] In this time of great uncertainty, when the safety of one's nearest and dearest was an ever-increasing concern, it was hardly surprising to find people turning to a movement that could promise that, if the worst happened, it was not, at least, the end.

Spiritualism, the belief that the spirits of the dead can communicate with the living, had been growing in popularity in Britain since the 1840s but exploded into the mainstream after the end of the Great War. There were an estimated 50,000 spiritualist circles established in the British Isles, and spiritualism became a recognised religion in the Armed Forces.[2] Significant numbers flocked to the churches professing that, not only had their loved ones survived when they crossed over, but that they had proof in the form of communication with them. This communication took place via a medium acting as an aid in creating a conduit between the dead and the living. With the advent of the Second World War came the return of fear and uncertainty for loved ones, especially in the chaos of the early years of fighting and the far-flung theatres of conflict from North Africa to the Far East. It is not surprising that a second surge of people sought out the help of mediums and it was clear that services offered by mediums filled a much-desired need.

There was, of course, another pressing preoccupation in wartime Britain: security or, more properly, propaganda – creating the illusion of security and the vital role of ordinary people in letting the State get on with prosecuting the war without asking questions.[3] With slogans such as 'Loose Lips Sink Ships' giving stark warning, anyone suspected of knowing or sharing too much would be closely monitored. It might not have been loose lips that sank the ship in 1941 however, but the lips of Helen Duncan. For the Scottish-born materialisation medium, who gained the rather telling nickname of Hellish Nell, named one particular ship as being sunk before anyone else, it was claimed, could possibly have known.

On 25 November 1941, the British Navy suffered a significant loss when the battleship *HMS Barham* was sunk by a German U-Boat. The tragedy occurred off the coast of Egypt and 861 men were lost, with only 395 rescued from the wreckage. The German vessel left the area too quickly to assess the damage inflicted knowing only that a British ship had been hit, not the devastating outcome. In the wake of the *Barham* tragedy, British Government policy changed; whereas prior to this incident the news of a sinking would have been released immediately, subsequently, news of the sinking was not only withheld from the British public, but also from the families of those who had lost their lives. The *Barham* was the last major British naval presence in the Mediterranean and when it became clear that the Germans were unaware of its sinking it was decided to keep the secret as long as possible.

During that same month, Helen Duncan held a séance at the Master Temple Psychic Centre at 301 Copnor Road, Southsea, Portsmouth. It was not as grand a place as it sounded, being merely the rooms above a pharmacy run by Ernest Homer and his wife, but the séance was well attended, with sixteen sitters to witness Helen's work. During the séance the form of a young sailor had appeared, wearing, it was said, a hat with '*HMS Barham*' clear on the hatband. The forlorn figure informed a woman in the audience that his ship, the *HMS Barham*, had been sunk and that many had died.

Many versions of what actually took place in the ensuing exchange have been recorded, with the woman involved reported as either the mother or wife of the returned seaman. However, all versions establish that the ship had been sunk, and when the woman protested that she had not been notified of the tragedy, the figure replied that she shortly would be, much to the consternation of all.

It is unknown whether Helen thought much of that moment over the following three years. Britain remained at war and many more ships were sunk. The story of one sailor at the beginning of the war must have faded from memory given the seemingly relentless losses that came after. Then, in January 1944, Helen was again due to travel to Portsmouth. She had been booked for a series of sittings at the Master Temple, the numbers of séance attenders in the bustling city port making the journey well worth her while. The night before she was to leave however, Helen's daughter Gena woke from a disturbing dream. In great distress, Gena was insistent that her mother should not make the journey, but her warnings went unheeded and Helen set off as planned little realising that she was about to enter the biggest drama of her life.

Whether Gena's warnings played on Helen's mind is not recorded, but her daughter was not the only one to express concern about this trip. Albert, Helen's spirit control, warned Mr and Mrs Homer that they were not to allow entrance to a man wearing naval uniform who would come to attend a séance during that week.[4] Albert's warning was, like Gena's, disregarded and a man in naval uniform – Stanley Worth – attended. He had been present for several previous séances at the Master Temple and, on the afternoon of 14 January, Worth arrived for the séance, as did another man, Surgeon Lieutenant Elijah Fowler.

There were about twenty people sitting that afternoon and Worth, at least, was less than impressed by what he experienced. True, his 'aunt' had appeared but as far as he was concerned, all of his aunts were alive and well, leaving him somewhat unimpressed by Helen's 'powers'. There were several other materialisations: young Peggy, a frequent visitor to Helen's séances, sang for those gathered and also, more bizarrely, the spirits of a parrot named Bronco, a cat and a rabbit.[5] Worth remained less than convinced of the authenticity of the séance and paid a visit to the police the following day. After consultation with Detective Inspector Ford of Portsmouth, a plan was hatched that would put Helen in grave danger.

Worth booked a further two seats for a séance on Wednesday 19 January at a cost of 25s. Rupert Cross, a War Reserve Constable and Worth's friend, accompanied him and, despite another warning from the usually less alarmist Albert, the two men were admitted to the séance room.[6] There were about thirty sitters that night and the séance began much the same as any other: Helen went into a trance and the group were led in the Lord's Prayer, followed by the singing of a song. The first couple of materialisations carried on without incident but, as the third came, events took an unexpected turn.

There are many versions of what happened next, but all agree that it was complete chaos. A loose sketch of events reveals that Cross leapt out of his seat and the cabinet curtains were thrust open, either on purpose or as he fell against them. It was reported that Helen was plainly seen trying to hide what appeared to be a length of material by pushing it up under her black séance dress.[7] A brief scuffle ensued as both parties attempted to gain possession of the 'cloth' with Worth shining his torch before it got knocked from his grasp. The cloth, if indeed that's what it was, vanished from sight – some say into the audience, whilst others believed it to have behaved like the ectoplasm it surely was by returning whence it came.

After struggling to put on her shoes, (or, in another version of the tale, with one of her shoes having come off) Helen started to shout, demanding the attentions of a doctor. Worth blew his whistle, and Ford and the three detectives who had been waiting outside with him burst onto the scene. The lights were turned on and a search made for the elusive sheet or cloth, to no avail.[8]

The outcome of the kerfuffle was that Helen was arrested under the Vagrancy Act, for 'pretending to hold communication with the spirits of deceased persons.'[9] Section Four of the 1824 Vagrancy Act stated that 'Every person pretending or professing to tell fortunes or using any subtle craft, means or device, by palmistry or otherwise, to deceive or impose on any of his Majesty's subjects ... shall be deemed a rogue or vagabond.'[10]

By the time the case finally came to court in March 1944 the charges had been altered slightly, and disastrously for Helen, as she was now to be charged under the Witchcraft Act of 1736, which stated that anyone pretending 'to exercise or use any kind of witchcraft, sorcery, enchantment or conjuration' was guilty.[11] The penalty for this crime was twelve months' imprisonment. Helen's trial began on Thursday 23 March at the Old Bailey, London's oldest criminal court, and was of great public interest. Standing accused with Helen were Ernest and Elizabeth Homer (who turned out to not be his wife after all) and Francis Brown, Helen's travelling companion. Lasting for seven days, the trial saw over thirty witnesses called for the defence, as Charles Loseby, Helen's defence solicitor, did his best not only to acquit Helen and her fellow accused but also, fatally, to prove the truth of existence after death.

Despite the overwhelming support for Helen and the tireless efforts of Loseby, on 31 March, Helen and her fellow accused were found guilty, with the jury taking just twenty-four minutes to reach their verdict. Sentencing took place on Monday 3 April, when the Homers were bound over for two years, whilst Francis Brown was sentenced to four months in prison. The harshest sentence was reserved for Helen; a custodial sentence of nine months, her shouts that she had done nothing wrong being to no avail. She was 46 at the time, wife to Henry Duncan, and mother of six.[12]

Although the message had been misunderstood when it came through, Helen's supporters had actually been forewarned of this disastrous outcome. At a meeting at the Bonnington Hotel on 30 March, Helen had been encouraged to partake in some direct writing and the following message was delivered: 'Two will be convicted and two will go free.'[13] Much to Helen's horror, however, it was the Homers who were to walk free that day while she returned to Holloway Prison to serve her sentence. Even at the time there were many who could scarcely believe that a custodial sentence was necessary for a woman of her age and the crime of which she had been convicted.

The reason for Helen's imprisonment has been much debated. The most obvious reason is that she was guilty as charged and had defrauded those who paid to attend the séance at Copnor Road; that the authorities truly believed her to be a menace and were set on making an example of her. After all, she was not the only medium to be prosecuted in the twentieth century, and as late as 1949, thirty-nine fortune tellers were prosecuted under the Vagrancy Act.[14] There were also many others who attended séances however, spreading the spiritualist message and working tirelessly to promote the cause with many prominent and high-profile people among them. Why did Helen then bear the brunt of the authorities' displeasure?

It was not the first time Helen had been in trouble with the law. On a previous occasion in January 1933 she had been arrested in Edinburgh when her powers were brought into question following a séance conducted for Miss Esson Maule.[15] It seems that contact between the Duncans and Maule had occurred as early as March 1932; Helen had performed séances after being booked by Maule, and it was after dissatisfaction with these that Maule decided to expose Helen for a fraud.[16] On 6 January, several spirits appeared as usual but the drama started when 'Peggy' materialised. Peggy was apparently, quite clearly Helen on her knees with something white being held before her and impersonating a childlike voice.[17] Maule asked the girl if she could shake her hand and when the figure drew close enough Maule grabbed at it, declaring she would see what she was made of. A tug of war ensued in which Maule testified that she was aware of stretching material being pulled sharply away from her. Helen won, but not before Maule's finger caught in the substance and tore a hole in it. Even more damningly, the curtains were pulled apart to reveal Helen frantically pushing a white garment up her dress, some of which was still clearly visible.

In the ensuing fracas, Helen swore and shouted in response to Maule's gleeful pronouncement that she had been caught out in fraud, declaring Maule a liar and threatening to kill her. She finally agreed to undress in front of the women sitters, but clearly under duress. The police were called and when they arrived, Maule wasted no time telling them that Helen had not only defrauded people but had also threatened her. Helen appeared in court to answer the charge of fraud, namely that she had pretended to eight people that she was a medium through whom deceased persons regularly materialised, and that if they attended her séance and paid 10s, the dead would materialise to them. Helen pleaded not guilty. The eventual verdict of the allegation of fraud was 'not proven' and Helen was made to pay a fine of £10, for disrupting the peace and use of bad language.[18]

The authorities were, therefore, aware of Helen's activities and it could have simply been that her luck had run out. The harshness of the sentence and use of the 1736 Act does, however, lead to speculation that there was another aspect at work. After all, Helen could have likewise been found guilty under the Vagrancy Act, and it does seem that there was a concerted effort made to ensure that her sentence resulted in imprisonment. Even this could be excused if Helen were making a nuisance of herself with séances and taking money from those whom, many felt, could ill afford it through being taken in by the act at the Master Psychic Temple.

The incompetence of Helen's defence lawyer, Charles Loseby, has also been cited as a reason for the guilty verdict. Instead of simply defending Helen from the charge against her, Loseby set out to defend spiritualism itself. Many believe that it was the admission of the previous offence into the Old Bailey trial coupled with Loseby's inexperience and youth that were responsible for his lacklustre defence. Malcolm Gaskill however, points out that Loseby was actually 62 and an experienced lawyer in his own right, meaning much of the criticism levelled at him is unjustified.[19] Nevertheless, the number of witnesses for the defence that were called in dragged the trial out so that, by the end of it all, the recorder and judge were clearly wearying of those speaking on Helen's behalf. There was also criticism that Helen herself was not called to speak, with Mr Homer being the only one of the accused to take the stand.

Another theory is that the authorities believed she had genuine powers due to her knowledge of the sinking of the *Barham* in 1941 and considered her a threat to security. Helen had form when it came to foretelling the fate of British ships; during a séance in Edinburgh in 1941, Helen announced that a ship had gone down. At this point, even the Admiralty were unaware that the *HMS Hood* had been blown up that day leaving only three survivors from a crew of 1,422. Brigadier Roy Firebrace, Chief of Military Intelligence for

Scotland and a supporter of Helen, had been attending the séance and rang the admiralty for confirmation. When they rang back to demand to know how he had discovered the information before they had, he revealed that it had been at a séance held by Helen Duncan.[20] When Lieutenant Worth approached Detective Inspector Ford in January 1944, he was probably already aware of Helen's connection with a prior dangerous security breach.

There are some who believe that Helen was persecuted because of the fear that she would unveil other, more important military secrets. The coincidence of the timing of Helen's arrest with the forthcoming D-Day landings has been given as a reason for official determination to have her out of the way. Her regular travel between Edinburgh and Portsmouth, two locations of great strategic importance in the run-up to D-Day, very possibly helped raise suspicions against her.[21]

Today, debate regarding Helen tends to hinge on whether she was, as she and her supporters claimed, a conduit between the two worlds or– as her detractors would have – nothing but a charlatan and a fraud. In this way, the *Barham* incident is critical. That there was a séance in which a sailor was reported to have appeared is beyond dispute, but the information imparted is open to interpretation. While there were many who had no doubt that the tale was true, it has been argued that the materialisation had been vague about his identity, the name *Barham* being uttered only when led by a member of the audience. The 'fact' that the hatband read *Barham* also points to either a deliberate act of fraud or some later exaggeration of the tale as, in wartime, the hat would have only had *HMS* on it for security reasons. Although news of the sinking of the *Barham* was not released officially until January 1942, a full two months after the incident occurred, there were many ways in which the information could have leaked such as from those who returned or other, unofficial, channels.[22] Finally, the loss of ships in wartime was not, unfortunately, an infrequent occurrence and it is possible that, in this case, a vague pronouncement from Helen had disastrous consequences. She may not even have foretold the news at all, the story becoming embellished after the fact.

Helen's staunchest critic was Harry Price. Helen and Price first met when Helen was in London with her husband, where she had agreed to have tests conducted by the London Spiritualist Alliance; Price, as coincidence would have it, occupied rooms at the top of the LSA's premises. Due to differences with the LSA, Price was not invited to the demonstration, but he seized his chance in April 1931 when Henry Duncan offered him the chance of a séance with Helen. Price was so convinced of Helen's fraud that he included a chapter called *The Cheese-Cloth Worshippers* in his *Psychic Case Book* of 1933, in which he spoke scathingly of the 'cheesecloth mania' of 1931–2 where Helen and her abilities were all the rage. After poking fun at the gullibility of anyone who could believe in Helen's claims or performances, and making a somewhat underhand dig at her weight, Price went on to tear Helen and her case to shreds. He reached the conclusion that Helen was a regurgitator, concealing cheesecloth in her stomach that then formed the substance of her 'materialisations,' citing other examples of this 'art' to support his theory.[23]

There are several photographs in existence that were taken during Helen's sittings with Price and they do appear to be decidedly 'home made' though how such fakery could have been achieved in the strict conditions set by Price is not explained.[24] Price pointed out that a phantom 'hand' had in fact been a rubber glove, whilst the child 'Peggy' was, at least on this one occasion, a paper face cut from a magazine attached to the ubiquitous cheesecloth.[25] The samples of 'ectoplasm' from which Helen's materialisations were formed resembled the white of an egg that had been hardboiled. Further analysis confirmed that it was made up of: 'white of a new-laid egg, ferric chloride, phosphoric acid and stale urine mixed with gelatine, along with hot margaric acid from olive oil.'[26]

There were also suspicions that Price was indirectly involved with Helen's arrest in 1933 through his contact with Esson Maule. Helen and her family were insistent that Helen had been set up; the address for the séance venue was changed at the last minute from the Psychic Institute to Maule's own house next door, and the woman who booked the séance used an assumed name. Maule had also helped Price's research into regurgitation and had given him photographs.

Adding to the negative accounts of Helen are tales of her failing to deliver, with those attending her séances being left unsatisfied. It has been suggested that Helen bullied those attending to accept the materialisations that appeared, even if they were uncertain, and often grew red faced and argumentative if people quibbled. There were complaints, both verbal and written, that the materialisations were fake and a hoax, and that it was easy to see that they shared the same size and shape as Helen. There was the complaint of Miss Marjory Preston who mentioned the rather damning evidence of an Arab Sheik who was seen sticking on his beard.[27] At a Lancashire séance of twenty sitters, the session was described as lacklustre and feeling 'off'; a materialisation was clearly Helen wearing a sheet, and there was another incident where she stretched out her arm whilst holding some white material in a deliberate pretence.[28] At a sitting near Methyr Tydfil near the start of the war there had been another altercation over a sheet or cloth, with two men struggling with Helen for possession of a fabric that had been pulled from one of the materialised forms, and a statement was taken and signed by witnesses.[29]

Even those who supported Helen and expressed belief in her powers were showing concerns by the time of the Portsmouth séance. Mr John Lane believed that by this point, Helen's séances could not be taken as genuine examples of materialisation, though he questioned whether Helen was aware of this, and was worried that she might be unwittingly perpetrating fraud in an unknowing trance-like state.[30] It has been suggested that Helen had been carrying out too many séances with too many sitters so that both Helen and the quality of her work were suffering. Henry Duncan, Helen's staunchest supporter, was unsure at times whether his wife's phenomena were entirely legitimate, admitting to Harry Price that she was capable both of genuine acts but also of fraud.[31]

Despite all this, Helen had a devoted and loyal following who believed wholeheartedly in her ability to connect with the dead. Far from being the sort who might be expected to believe in anything, Helen's loudest support was from the most respected corners of society. Jane Rust, a widow and retired midwife, had sat with Helen on several occasions and had no doubts that Helen was genuine. She had seen both her husband and her mother appear before her, the latter with several distinguishing physical marks in the correct places. Most remarkable was the appearance of her Aunt Mary, who spoke the language she had used in life; Gibraltarian Spanish. In Jane Rust's own words, she had 'never been more certain of anything in my life before.'[32]

Then there was Wing Commander George Mackie who talked with both his mother and brother, the latter being recognisable by his distinctive handlebar moustache. Sir James Harris, JP, gave evidence concerning the appearance of none other than Sir Arthur Conan Doyle himself, a friend of his, who he had no trouble recognising when he materialised for about ten seconds and shared a brief, yet convincing, conversation. Vincent Woodcock found new love, thanks to Helen, with his sister-in-law. His wife appeared in séances nineteen times in the space of three years, recognisable by the palpitations that had killed her and the mention of the flowers their young daughter had brought to her funeral. On one memorable occasion, Woodcock's wife removed the wedding ring from her former husband's hand and placed it on her sister's finger.[33] Mrs Tremlett witnessed the materialisation of a man with the rather noticeable feature of a stump for one arm. She also cited much in the way of physical contact in the séance she attended, with handshakes and kisses that were, she was certain, from those who had passed over and not the medium playing 'bogey bogey' with a sheet as had been suggested.[34] Hannen Swaffer, a spiritualist and journalist who had achieved fame and notoriety, was decidedly outspoken during his time on the witness stand. He spoke at length regarding Helen and her abilities, describing the ectoplasm that flowed from Helen as being akin to white, living snow. When asked whether one might mistake a sheet or cloth for what he described, Swaffer was firm that only a child could be so confused. [35]

There are those who claim that Winston Churchill himself was a staunch supporter of Helen's. This theory is based on a memo written to the Home Secretary, where Churchill demanded:

Let me have a report on why the Witchcraft Act of 1735 was used in a modern Court of Justice.

What was the cost of the trial to the state, observing that witnesses were brought from Portsmouth and maintained here in this crowded London for a fortnight, and the Recorder kept busy with all this obsolete tomfoolery... [36]

From this, there have been various claims and theories put forward, one of the more extravagant being that the Prime Minister himself visited Helen when she was in prison. It is more likely however that he was simply objecting to the misuse of time and funds, rather than having a vested interest in the Spiritualist cause. The rumour that Churchill visited Helen comes from a misunderstanding. Churchill's daughter, Sarah, attended a séance of Helen's and then reported back to her father.

It was not only Helen's perceived abilities that divided opinion. There were equally opposing camps where character and appearance were concerned. It has already been mentioned that Helen was said to 'bully' sitters and there have been examples during her arrests where she is on record as having shouted and been violent. Her temper was well known, admitted even by Helen's daughter Gena in her decidedly sanitised version of her mother's life. Mrs Gray described Helen before a séance to be held in Paignton, Devon as 'A coarse and immensely fat woman, partly naked, … sitting on a chair smoking the fag end of a cigarette.'[37] She admitted that the very sight of the medium disgusted her, a revulsion that perhaps coloured her view of the séance to follow or, in another interpretation, allowed her to see around the showmanship, where she was very clear that Helen's materialisations were nothing more than the medium herself using various methods of disguise and subterfuge.

Despite such damning opinions, there were many who saw Helen as an angel on earth, providing support and help in their times of crisis. Helen was known for great acts of kindness, helping those who had very little, even when her own family was struggling financially.

After the trial at The Old Bailey, an unsuccessful appeal was made against the sentences of Helen and Frances Brown. Helen saw out her nine months in Holloway Prison, and was released on 22 September 1944. If indeed the authorities had been worried that Helen would leak information about the D-Day Landings such fears were unfounded; to this day the operation remains one of the most successfully kept secrets in military history.

Having declared that she would not go back to giving séances, Helen did however return to her work. During this time, and largely as a response to Helen's trial and the publicity it garnered for the spiritualist cause, moves were made in earnest to bring about changes to the legislation under which Helen had been charged. In both 1945 and 1950, parliamentary candidates were questioned as to their stance on reform with a heartening total of two hundred MPs intimating that they were in support of amendments.[38] As a consequence, the Fraudulent Mediums Act was passed on 22 June 1951 and witchcraft left English law for good.[39]

In October 1956, Henry Duncan woke in the middle of the night to see his wife standing at the end of their bed – this was surprising for two reasons: she was wearing her clothes, and she was supposed to be in Nottingham conducting a séance for a Mr Timmins. Helen explained, in some distress, that she had been about to leave him but had been unable to do so, then the vision disappeared, leaving Henry shaken and unable to return to sleep. Despite reassurances from Gena, the next morning a telegram arrived: Helen had been taken ill and Gert Hamilton, the friend who had travelled with her, was bringing her home to Edinburgh that day.

It was clear upon her return that Helen was in a bad way; she was shaking and unsteady, with two burns on her right breast and stomach. The séance, which had started typically enough, had descended into chaos when, twenty minutes in, the room was flooded by police. Amidst demands to see the fake beards and sheets that were, they were certain, used in her acts, Helen fell and appeared so ill that a doctor was summoned to administer insulin to stabilise the diabetic medium's condition. Helen was cautioned and released the following day, and it was then that Gert had sent the telegram and brought her home.

It was to be Helen's last séance. Although her condition stabilised, she remained ill, a stay in hospital doing little to help her either physically or mentally. Helen died, aged 59, in the early hours of 6 December; her kindness, along with the happiness and closure that she gave to many through her séances living on in the memories of those who had known her.

That was not, however, the last to be seen of Helen. There were also more tangible reminders of the woman who had been both loved and reviled by so many. A medium from Glasgow reportedly received a message from Helen on the day of her death, reassuring people that not only was she happy and reunited with her dead daughter Nan, but she had also been greeted by Albert and there was no cause for worry. Henry Duncan had an encounter with Helen appearing one night and taking his hand, something which calmed and cheered him greatly. Helen was also said to have materialised fully on several occasions during séances held by a medium named Rita Goold during the 1980s. In these cases Helen was said to act as a 'guide' and there were also occasions where objects were aported – i.e materialised from another place – including a red rose that appeared in the presence of Helen's daughter Gena and, most famously in 1994, the fiftieth anniversary of Helen's trial, a copy of the Daily Mail for 1 April 1944.[40]

Interest in Helen has not abated, her life and work the subject of many books and articles, with the naval investigation and subsequent trial dramatised as a radio play, *The Last Witch Trial* in 2010 and on-going plans afoot for a film of her story. There are also many today who believe Helen was wrongfully convicted and imprisoned and there have been several attempts to officially clear her name. The most recent, in 2008, failed when the Scottish Parliament refused to grant Helen the pardon that her supporters had campaigned for. This did not mark the end however and plans are currently in motion to restart the campaign, with questions to be put to the government regarding Helen's trial and the refusal to clear her name.

And so, as the last British witch, Helen remains a dividing and a unifying cause, bringing both peace and controversy to many, in death as she did in life.

Afterword

The last person to be convicted under the 1736 Witchcraft Act was Jane Rebecca Yorke on 26 September, 1944. She was charged with pretending to manifest spirits of the dead on seven instances, and was fined and bound over rather than given a custodial sentence due to her age.[1] Although nuisance mediums and fortune tellers would be targeted until the passing of the 1951 Fraudulent Mediums Act, never again would someone be sentenced as guilty under it.

Did belief in witches and their power over people likewise disappear with the passing of this new legislation? It must be remembered that witch beliefs are still strong in many areas of the world today, and people are still tortured and killed under the belief that they are guilty of bewitching those around them. Throughout the British Isles, the stereotypical witch is today generally seen as a figure of fun – prevalent around Halloween time, a character in a story book or a children's film – far removed from the individuals whose stories are contained in this book. Witchcraft has also seen a revival in recent times, with the reinvention and development of modern day Wicca and other movements reclaiming the concepts of witch and witchcraft for a more positive use. It is easy therefore to think of the superstitious past in a vacuum, far removed from the reason and enlightenment of modern times, but there are uncomfortable parallels if one is ready and willing to look. For although the witch is no longer present as a threat, other enemies from within have risen to take her place – immigrants and asylum seekers, those in receipt of benefits, the poor, the homeless, the needy to name but a few – now stand where the witch once stood. The group has changed, but the principal is still the same – the unfounded fear that there is a threat, lurking, waiting to rise up and consume all that is held dear. And like with witches, there is the belief that this threat must be dealt with, that these 'others' must be rooted out and made to pay. The fates of these eleven women perhaps come as a timely reminder, a call to examine our own views and prejudices as we take on the role of accuser to their accused.

That stark reflection of our times, Rebecca Lenkiewicz's *Jane Wenham: The Witch of Walkern*, again comes to mind here, when, towards the end of the play, a character asks:

"Where does all the hate hereabouts come from?"

Her companion's response is perhaps the most revealing of all, as he responds:

"People are unhappy. Jealous. They enjoy another's suffering."

He then adds the ultimate question; tinged with a disbelief that we should share, as we question and examine the all-too-ready willingness of people to turn against one another even in these 'enlightened' times:

"Unless they truly believe it all.
Do they?"[2]

Perhaps there is a lesson in this, one that we would do well to learn before it is too late.

Select Bibliography

Anderson, Michael, *British Population History From the Black Death to the Present Day*, Cambridge, Cambridge University Press 1996.

Anonymous, The Wonderful Discovery of the Witchcrafts of Margaret and Phillip Flower, London 1619.

Anonymous, *Signs and Wonders from Heaven*, London 1644.

Anonymous, *The Lawes against Witches and Conjuration and Some brief Notes and Observations for the Discovery of Witches*, London 1645.

Anonymous, *The Witch of Wapping or an Exact and Perfect Relation of the Life and Devilish Practices of Joan Peterson*, London 1652.

Anonymous, *The Case of the Hertfordshire Witchcraft Consider'd*, London 1712.

Barger, George, *Ergot and Ergotism*, London, Gurney and Jackson 1931.

Bedfordshire and Luton Archives Service, *The Parish Register for Milton Ernest 1538–1812*.

Borman, Tracy, *Witches: A Tale of Sorcery, Scandal and Seduction*, London, Random House 2013.

Bragge, Francis, *A Defence of the Proceedings against Jane Wenham*, London 1712.

Bragge, Francis, *A Full and Impartial Account of the Discovery of Sorcery and Witchcraft, Practis'd by Jane Wenham of Walkern*, London 1712.

Bragge, Francis, *Witchcraft father display'd*, London 1712.

Brealey, Gena, *The Two Worlds of Helen Duncan*, York, Saturday Night Press 2008.

Briggs, Robin, *Witches and Neighbours*, New York, Penguin 1996.

Browne, Philip, *The History of Norwich*, Norwich 1814.

Cabell Craig, *Witchfinder General: The Biography of Matthew Hopkins*, Stroud, The History Press 2006.

Carr, A. D, *The Mostyns of Mostyn 1540–1642*, Flintshire Historical Society Journal, Volume 28, 1977–1978.

Cassrier, Manfred, *Medium on Trial: The Story of Helen Duncan and The Witchcraft Act*, Essex, PN Publishing 1996.

Clarke, G R, *The History and Description of the Town and Borough of Ipswich*, London, 1830.

Cockburn, J.S. (ed), *Calendar of Assize Records: Essex Indictments Elizabeth I*, London, Stationary Office1978.

Coohill, Joseph, *Ireland: A Short History History*, London, Oneworld Publications 2014.

Cotta, John, *A Short Discoverie of the Unobserved Dangers*, London, 1612.

Cowan, Edward J and Henderson, Lizanne, *Scottish Fairy Belief A History*, Dundurn 2001.

Cox, Rev J Charles, *Three Centuries of Derbyshire Annals*, London, Bemrose 1890.

Crawford, Patricia, Mendelson Sara, *Women in Early Modern England*, Oxford, Clarendon 1998.

Curran, Bob, *A Bewitched Land: Ireland's Witches*, Dublin, O'Brien Press 2005.

Curtis, Edmund, *A History of Irelan,*: London, Methuen 1936.

Davidson, L.S, Ward, J.O, *The Sorcery Trial of Alice Kyteler*, North Carolina, Pegasus Press 2004.

Davies, Owen, *Witchcraft, Magic and Culture 1736–1951*, Manchester University Press 1999.

Davies, Owen, *Popular Magic: Cunning Folk in English History*, London, Continuum 2007.

Davies, Owen, *A People Bewitche*d, David and Charles, 2012.

Davies, R. T, *Four Centuries of Witch Beliefs*, London, Routledge 2011.

Deacon, Richard, *Matthew Hopkins Witch Finder General*, London, Anchor Press 1976.

Defoe, Daniel, *The Political History of the Devil*, London, 1727.

Derbyshire Record Office, *Q/SB/2/170, Quarter Sessions Document, Information of Francis Torratt Against Anne Wagg.*

Egan, P.M, *The Keteller Monument, Kilkenny*: The Journal of the Royal Society of Antiquaries of Ireland, Fifth Series, Vol. 5, No. 1. March 1895.

Ewen, C. L'Estrange, ed, *Witch Hunting and Witch Trials*, London, Kegan Paul, Trench, Trubner & Co. 1929.

Ewen, C. L'Estrange ed, *Witchcraft and Demonism*, London, Heath Cranton 1933.

Exeter and Plymouth Gazette, 13 March, 1852; 24 April 1852; 6 October, 1860.

Fawrar, Janet and Stewart, *Spells and How They Work*, London, Robert Hale 2010.

Fletcher, Anthony, *Gender, Sex and Subordination in England, 1500–1800*, Newhaven and London, Yale 1999.

Flinders, Stephen and Heather, ed. *Ilkeston St.Marys The Parish Registers 1588–1699.*

Flinders, Stephen, *Ilkeston Families of the 16th and 17th Centuries. Volume I*: Derbyshire, 2007.

Gaskill, Malcolm, *Hellish Nell Last of Britain's Witches*, London, Fourth Estate 2001.

Gaskill, Malcolm, *Witchfinders: A Seventeenth-Century English Tragedy*, London, John Murray Publishers 2006.

Gaskill, Malcolm, *Witchcraft: A Very Short Introduction*, Oxford, Oxford University Press 2010.

Gibson, Marion, *Early Modern Witches: Witchcraft Cases in Contemporary Writing*, London, Routledge, 2000.

Gibson, Marion, ed, *Witchcraft and Society in England and America, 1550–1750*, New York, Cornell University Press 2003.

Gilbert, J.T, *History of the Viceroys of Ireland*, London, J. Duffy 1865.

Goodare, Julian, *Women and the Witch Hunt in Scotland:* Social History Vol. 23, No. 3, Oct, 1998.

Goodare, Julian, Martin,Lauren, Miller, Joyce, and Yeoman, Louise, *'The Survey of Scottish Witchcraft'*,http://www.shca.ed.ac.uk/witches/(archived January 2003, accessed '20/9/2015').

Grace, James, *Annales Hiberniae*, Irish Archaeological Society 1842.

Guskin, Phyllis J, *The Context of Witchcraft: The Case of Jane Wenham (1712)*, Eighteenth-Century Studies, Vol 15, No 1, Autumn, 1981.

Henderson, L, *Witch-hunting and witch belief in the Gaidhealtachd: Witchcraft and Belief in Early Modern Scotland*, Palgrave Macmillan 2008.

Hatton, Jean, *George Fox: A Biography of the Founder of the Quakers*, Oxford, Monarch Books 2007.

Hertfordshire Archives and Local Studies, Walkern, DP/114/1/2 Baptism December 1679, Elizabeth Cooke.

Hertfordshire Archives and Local Studies, Walkern, *DP/114/1/2 Baptism December 1681, Sarah Cooke.*

Hertfordshire Archives and Local Studies, Walkern, *DP/114/1/1 Burial of Phillip Cook/Cooke 1696.*

Hertfordshire Archives and Local Studies, Walkern, *DP/114/1/2 Marriage of Jane Cooke and Edward Wenham, 1697.*

HMC, *The Manuscripts of His Grace the Duke of Rutland, Preserved at Belvoir Castle, Vol IV,* London, 1905.

Honeybone, Michael, *Wicked Practise and Sorcerye – The Belvoir Witchcraft case of 1619*, Buckingham, Baron Books 2008.

Hutchinson, Francis, *An Historical Essay Concerning Witchcraft*, London 1718.

Hutton, William, *The History of Derby*, London, J. Nichols 1817.

Ilkeston Local Studies Library, *Waterhouse MSS 50a, Ilkeston Manor Court Rolls.*

James I, *Daemonologie*: London, 1603.

Jennings, Pete, *Haunted Ipswich*, Stroud, The History Press 2010.

Jones, David L, *The Ipswich Witch: Mary Lackland and the Suffolk Witch Hunts*, Stroud, The History Press 2015.

Kerr, Margaret H, *Cold Water and Hot Iron: Trial by Ordeal in England*: The Journal of Interdisciplinary History Vol. 22, No. 4, Spring, 1992.

Killeen, Richard, *Ireland: Land, People, History*, Constable and Robinson 2012.

Kingsbury, J.B, *The Last Witch of England*, Folklore, Vol 61, No 3 Sep. 1950.

Larner, Christina, *Enemies of God: The Witch-hunt in Scotland*, Oxford, Basil Blackwell 1983.

Laurence, Anne, *Women in England 1500–1760*, London, Phoenix Press 2002.

Macfarlane, Alan, *Witchcraft in Tudor and Stuart England, London*, Routledge 1999.

Mackerell, Benjamin, *The History and Antiquities of the Flourishing Corporation of Kings Lynn*: Norwich, 1738.

Maxwell-Stuart, P.G, *Witch Hunters*, Stroud, Tempus 2003.

Maxwell-Stuart, P.G, *The Great Scottish Witch-Hunt*, Stroud, Tempus 2007.

Maxwell-Stuart, P.G, *The British Witch: The Biography*, Stroud, Amberley 2014.

McCurrach, M, *Freemen of the Borough of Ipswich part Two*: Suffolk Family History Society, 2000.

Meek, C. E and Simms M. K. (ed), *The Fragility of Her Sex – Medieval Irish Women in Their European Context*, Dublin, Four Courts Press 1996.

Mortensen, Jennifer, *Bottesford Parish Register Transcripts*. www.leicestershire.webs. com and www.parishchest.com.

Murray, Margaret Alice, *The Witch-Cult in Western Europe*, Oxford, Clarendon 1921.

Murtagh, Anne and Patterson, Tony, *Stepping Into Kilkenny's History*, Kilkenny Education Centre.

National Library of Wales, *Great Sessions Records. 4/9/4 10–15, 34, 55, 56*.

Newman, David, *The Importance of Milton Ernest*, Bedfordshire, ME Publications 2006.

Nolan, William and Whelan Kevin, (ed), *Kilkenny: History and Society. Interdisciplinary Essays on the History of an Irish County*, Geography Publications 1990.

North Devon Journal, 29 April, 1852.

Notestein, Wallace, *A History of Witchcraft in England from 1558–1718*, Baltimore, Lord Baltimore Press 1911.

Odingsells, Charles, *Two Sermons, Lately preached at Langar in the Valley of Belvoir*, London, 1620.

Parkin, Sally, *Witchcraft, women's honour and customary law in early modern Wales*, Social History Vol 31 No. 3 August 2006.

Penney, Norman, ed, *The Journal of George Fox*, Cambridge, Cambridge University Press,1911.

Pitcairn, Robert, *Ancient Criminal Trials in Scotland*, Edinburgh, William Tait and Longman 1833.

Price, Harry, *Leaves from a Psychist's Case-Book*, London, Victor Gollancz 1933.

Prim, John G.A, *Notes on Kilkenny Inns and Taverns*: The Kilkenny and South East of Ireland Archaeological Society, 1862.

Pugh, Roy J. M, *The Devl's Ain*, Harlaw Heritage 2001.

Puttick, Betty, *Ghosts of Suffolk*, Berkshire, Countryside Books 2004.

Redstone, Vincent Burrough, *Memorials of Old Suffolk*, London, Bemrose and Sons 1908.

Riddell, William Renwick, *Post-Reformation Burning at the Stake of Heretics*, Journal of the American Institute of Criminal Law and Criminology, Vol 21, No. 2, August 1930.

Roberts, C.E. Bechhofer, *The Trial of Mrs Duncan*, London, Jarrolds 1945.

Ross, David R, *Women of Scotland*, Edinburgh, Luath Press Limited 2010.

Serpell, James A, *Guardian Spirits or Demonic Pets: The Concept of the Witch's Familiar in Early Modern England, 1530–1712*: The Animal/Human Boundary: Rochester, NY: Rochester University Press 2002.

Seymour, John. D, *Irish Witchcraft and Demonology*, Dublin, Hodges, Fidge & Co. 1913.

Shandler, Nina, *The Strange Case of Hellish Nell*, Cambridge, MA, Da Capo Press 2006.

Snell, F. J, *The Customs of Old England*, Reprint, 2015.

Stevenson, Jason, *The Barham Conspiracy*, World War II Magazine, December, 2004.

Stone, Brian. Derbyshire in the Civil War, Derbyshire, Scarthin Books 1992.

Stone, Lawrence, *Uncertain Unions and Broken Lives*, Oxford, Oxford University Press 1995.

Suffolk Record Office, Bury. *SROB C8/4/7, Sessions of the Peace, Borough of Ipswich 1645.*

Suggett, Richard, *Witchcraft in Early Modern Wales*: Women and Gender in Early Modern Wales, Cardiff, University of Wales Press 2000.

Suggett, Richard, *A History of Magic and Witchcraft in Wales*, Stroud, The History Press 2008.

Taunton Courier, and Western Advertiser, 18 July, 1860.

The True Informer, 23rd July 1645.

Thomas, Keith, *Religion and the Decline of Magic*, London, Penguin, 1991.

Thompson, Richard, *Illustrations of the History of Great Britain Volume I*, Edinburgh, Constable and Co. 1828.

Throsby, John, *The Supplementary Volume to the Leicestershire Views: Containing a Series of Excursions in the Year 1790, to the Villages and Places of Note in the County*, London, J. Nichols 1790.

Trueman, Edwin, *History of Ilkeston*, John F. Walker 1880.

Walker-Meikle, Kathleen, *Medieval Pets*, Woodbridge, The Boydell Press 2012.

Western Times, Supplement, Exeter. 14 July, 1860.

White, Edward, *A Detection of Damnable Driftes*, London, 1579.

White, William, *History, Gazetteer, and Directory of Devonshire*, Simkin, Marshall and Company 1850.

Wilby, Emma, *The Visions of Isobel Gowdie*: Magic, Witchcraft and Dark Shamanism in Seventeenth-Century Scotland, Sussex, Sussex Academic Press 2013.

Williams, J. Gwynn, *Witchcraft in Seventeenth-Century Flintshire*, Journal of the Flintshire Historical Society, 1975–1976.

Wodderspoon, John, *A New Guide to Ipswich*, Ipswich, J.M. Burton 1842.

Worden, Blair, *The English Civil Wars 1640–1660*, London, W&N 2010.

Wynter. P (ed), *The Works of Joseph Hall*, Oxford, D.A Talboys 1863.

Zupko, Ronald Edward, *Dictionary of Weights and Measures for the British Isles: The Middle Ages To the Twentieth Century*, Philadelphia, American Philosophical Society 1985.

Notes

Introduction

1. Gaskill, Malcolm *Witchcraft: A Very Short Introduction* (Oxford University Press 2010) p.76. Most current estimates rest around this number, with Brian P Levack suggesting 60,000 to adjust for those lost or unrecorded. Much higher figures have been suggested in the past and by a few modern historians but the general consensus is that these are much exaggerated.
2. Goodare, Julian; Martin, Lauren; Miller, Joyce; and Yeoman, Louise, *The Survey of Scottish Witchcraft*, http://www.shca.ed.ac.uk/witches/ (archived January 2003, accessed 20/9/2015).

Chapter 1

1. Killeen, Richard, *Ireland:Land, People, History* (Constable and Robinson, 2012) p.56. The first Norman incursion from the newly-conquered England reached Ireland in 1169. It was not until Henry II landed in Waterford in October 1171 however that England could be said to have "arrived" in the country. The years that followed saw the growth of English might and power, only to decline again under Edward II, heralding a period of hostilities between the colonists and the native Gaelic population. There is debate over whether English Lordship was every fully restored after this point, with some arguing that the defeat of the invasion of Edward Bruce was the beginning of the end, whilst other sources argue that this in fact marked the restoration of English power in Ireland. For more on the subject see Killeen, *Ireland: Land, People, History* and Curtis, Edmund *A History of Ireland* (Methuen 1936).
2. William Outlawe, Alice's first husband after whom her son was named, had been a wealthy merchant, and Alice would have received a widow's portion at the death of her husband, increasing the wealth inherited from her own father. It is unclear when Outlawe died, but records show that Alice was married to Adam le Blund by 1302. Another money-lender, le Blund left all of his wealth to his step-son William in 1307, causing great resentment, especially from his children from a previous marriage. Again dates are hazy, but Alice had remarried again by 1309, only for her third husband, Richard de Valle to die around 1316. At this time Alice had to sue her step-son in order to gain her widow's portion to which she was legally entitled.

3. On 29 November, 1317 the Bishop held his first synod, at which several canons were passed. One is of particular note as it sets out clearly Ledrede's views on the situation in his new diocese: 'Alone however, a certain pestiferous new outgrowth in some of our regions, in contrast with the other faiths of the earth, full of the spirit of the Devil, cutting itself off from the persuasion of all worshippers of God, more cruel than gentiles and Jews, deserving the Lord's curse, harasses both in life and death the bishops and priests of the supreme God by despoiling and devastating the patrimony of Christ in the diocese of Ossory. We are compelled, insofar as we are able, to remedy their wicked acts which have increased and become stronger than usual.' Constitutions of Ossory, Canon 15, in Davidson L.S and Ward J.O *The Sorcery Trial of Alice Kyteler* (Pegasus Press, 2004) p.77.

4. Alice's son William called on two powerful men – Lord Arnold le Poer, seneschal of Kilkenny (and probably a relative of Alice's fourth and currently ailing husband) and the chancellor himself, Roger Outlawe (probably uncle to William himself) to come to his mother's aid.

5. The seneschal was the representative of the lord of each liberty or county, and performed the role of the highest judge and official there in his stead.

6. Davidson and Ward, *The Sorcery Trial of Alice Kyteler* p.33.

7. Ledrede is quoted as saying 'This day should not be a day of grief and sorrow for you, but rather a day of joy and gladness, for this imprisonment for faith in Christ will bring us greater honour than anything else we have ever done in our whole life, excepting only the sacrament of baptism and the ceremony of consecration.' Davidson and Ward, *The Sorcery Trial of Alice Kyteler.* p.39.

8. Refusing and citing worries for his safety whilst passing through lands owned by Lord Arnold, the Bishop instead offered to appear at the court the seneschal was holding at Kilkenny at that time. The offer was rudely rebuffed, the message being sent to the bishop that he would enter the court at his own peril. Unperturbed, Ledrede turned up, in full vestments with his entourage where, amidst much reluctance, he was finally admitted. Arnold made his feelings on the matter very clear indeed, referring to Ledrede scathingly as 'that ignorant, lowborn tramp from England'. (The term had a different meaning from that in use today and implied a monk who had left his monastery or a cleric who had abandoned his parish, and was intended as an insult towards Ledrede for leaving England to intrude on Irish affairs.) Ledrede finally left to much uproar after the seneschal told him in no uncertain terms that he would not support Ledrede's quest against Alice and her associates. *The Sorcery Trial of Alice Kyteler*, p.45.

9. *Ibid*, p.48.

10. Arnold, with the power and wherewithal to do so, ordered that Ledrede's officers be arrested.

11. The period of time to abstain for would vary, depending on the size or importance of the matter wished to be granted. It could range from anything from a few days to a whole year.

12. This demon appeared in various forms, sometimes as a dog or cat, and sometimes as a man with black skin who came with two companions.

13. After intercession from the chancellor and the treasurer, Outlawe's sentence was commuted to saying three masses every day for a year, feeding the poor in the town and re-covering the roof of Canice's cathedral in lead at his own expense.

14. By her own admission Petronilla had made sacrifices to demons on three occasions at Alice's instigation. She had also, along with her mistress, denied Christ and his church and had been witness on at least one occasion as Alice and the demon Robin knew each other carnally.

15. Petronilla de Meath thus entered history as the first person to be executed for witchcraft in Ireland. It was also claimed by John Clyn in his chronicles that she was the first to be executed for heresy in that country, stating that 'Moreover, before her, even in the olden days, it was neither seen nor heard of that anyone suffered the death penalty for heresy in Ireland.' Extract from Clyn, John *Annales Hiberniae* in Davidson and Ward, *The Sorcery Trial of Alice Kyteler.* p.80.

16. There has been little speculation regarding Alice's journey, but the most likely place for her to have sailed from would be Dublin, her destination either England or onwards to return to the Flemish origins of her ancestors.

17. *Patent Roll 31 Edward I* (1303) in *The Sorcery Trial of Alice Kyteler*, p.85.

18. *Ibid.* p.85.

19. Family politics in general were in no way clear cut. A William Kyteler, sheriff of Kilkenny, was involved in the allegations against Alice and Adam le Blund in 1303 and, despite John le Poer's belief against his wife, it was the seneschal Arnold le Poer, who was her staunchest supporter.

20. Thomas, Keith, *Religion and the Decline of Magic* (Penguin, 1991) p.528.

21. *The Sorcery Trial of Alice Kyteler.* p.29. The demon who featured most prominently in the accusations against Alice and Petronilla's confession, went by the name of Robin or Robert, Son of Art. As a spirit familiar summoned to do her bidding, he is referred to in the accusations as her incubus – a male demon who had sexual intercourse with a sleeping woman. It was from this demon that Alice got her power, and it was him she had to thank for her wealth and possessions. One interpretation of this is that Alice had been involved in an affair or affairs, and that the 'demon' was actually a lover.

Although the sexual link between witches and demons was new, the belief that demons had sexual relations with humans was not; both St. Augustine and Thomas Aquinas make reference to it and it is possible therefore that the reference in Alice's case was an extension of these pre-existing beliefs. Maxwell-Stuart, P.G. *The British Witch: The Biography* (Amberley, 2014) p.47.

22. *The Sorcery Trial of Alice Kyteler,* p.63.

23. Silverman, Maida *A City Herbal* (Ash Tree Publishing, 1997) pp. 162–68 Also known under many other names such as Achillea millefoilum, (after Achilles

who supposedly healed the wounds of his soldiers with this herb) yarrow or arrow root and, more evocatively, Devil's nettle it was well known for stopping the flow of blood, cleaning a wound and was also used to stop internal bleeding. The flowers being the most beneficial part of the plant, it can also help stomach and liver complaints, and help remove toxins from the body. Its odour is 'pungent' and tastes bitter. As well as the clearly beneficial uses, the herb had a long association with witchcraft and magic, and could also be used as a protective counter-measure.

24. Maxwell-Stuart, *The British Witch* p.53.
25. This was a great deal in part due to the recent destruction of the Templars. It has been argued that Ledrede drew connections between the apostasy, worship of demons and belief that their wealth came from Baphomet whom they worshipped and the details in the Kyteler case. *ibid* p.49.
26. John Seymour in his 1913 *Irish Witchcraft and Demonology* believed that 'The lady in question must have been far removed from the popular conception of a witch as an old woman of striking ugliness, or else her powers of attraction were very remarkable, for she had succeeded in leading four Husbands to the altar.' (p. 26.) Bob Curran follows suit with his assertion that Alice was 'in all likelihood quite a handsome woman.' Curran, Bob *A Bewitched Land: Ireland's Witches* (O'Brien Press, 2005) p.20.
27. It has been suggested that Josef Kyteler may have been the father or grandfather of Alice. William Outlawe, Alice's only surviving son, is thought to have been born around the time of Josef's death.
28. Murtagh, Anne and Patterson, Tony, *Stepping Into Kilkenny's History* Kilkenny Education Centre.
29. Egan, P.M *The Keteller Monument, Kilkenny*, in *The Journal of the Royal Society of Antiquaries of Ireland, Fifth Series, Vol. 5, No. 1* (March 1895), p.78.
30. *Ibid.* p.76.
31. Prim, John G. A., *Notes on Kilkenny Inns and Taverns* in the Journal of The Kilkenny and South East of Ireland Archaeological Society (1862) p.155.
32. *Ibid* p.154.
33. Grace, James *Annales Hiberniae* (Irish Archaeological Society, 1842) p.101.
34. *Ibid* p.101.
35. Versions of these 'facts' can be found in James Grace's *Annales Hiberniae*, and Holinshed's *Chronicles of England, Scotland and Ireland*, among others.
36. One particularly illuminating assessment is that 'Alice appears to have been a partner with her son, and to have sought to accumulate money, not only by usury, and even by scavenging the streets, of Kilkenny, but by fortune-telling and trafficking in charms and piltres – a business of great profit during the then almost universal belief in dealings with demons and spirits.' Gilbert, J.T, *History of the Viceroys of Ireland* (1865) p.154.

37. Novels on Alice Kyteler include *The Burning Time*, Robin Morgan, 2006, *The Stone*, Clare Nolan, 2008, *The Devil to Pay*, Hugh Ryan Fitzgerald, 2010, *The Kyteler Witch*, Candace Muncy Poole, 2014.

38. For an exploration of this idea, see Puhvel, Martin, The Wyf of Bath and Alice Kyteler – A Web of Parallelism, Studia Neophilologica, vol 53, 1981.

Chapter 2

1. Serpell, James A, *Guardian Spirits or Demonic Pets: The Concept of the Witch's Familiar in Early Modern England, 1530–1712* The Animal/Human Boundary. ed. Creager, A.N.H. & Jordan, W.C. (Rochester, NY: Rochester University Press, 2002) p.160.

   A familiar was a spirit that did a witch's bidding and often appeared to help her once she had made the decision to enter into a life of witchcraft.

2. One argument is that these familiars were the English counterpart of the Devils who appeared in Continental trial reports, with the familiars mentioned in English witchcraft accounts representing or even taking on the role of the Devil. With the witch entering into a compact or bargain with the familiar, the animal quite literally became "the container or cipher for the witch's own desires and anger." Briggs, Robin *Witches and Neighbours* (Penguin, 1998) pp29–30.

3. This is not particularly surprising as they were a popular pet during the sixteenth century. Cats in general have had a long and chequered history and the frequency with which they were named as familiars is unsurprising. One of the charges against the Templars involved worship of a cat, and it was rumoured that the Cathars not only worshipped the Devil in the form of a black cat, but also that the very name of their sect came from that source. Cats were popular pets (a term that only came into usage in the sixteenth century) but their status was not quite straightforward as they were kept not only for companionship but also to perform the task of keeping down mice, being both domesticated and wild. Walker-Meikle, Kathleen, *Medieval Pets* (The Boydell Press, 2014) p10–14.

4. This was a term used to refer to dysentery; a painful infection that led to the inflammation of the intestines. Symptoms included bloody stools, diarrhoea, fever, painful cramping and general weakness. It was a common yet potentially deadly ailment at the time and caused the deaths of many. It is not clear whether Agnes was successful on this occasion.

5. Agnes' case would instead have been set aside for judgement once the other trials were finished. Gibson, Marion, *Early Modern Witches: Witchcraft Cases in Contemporary Writing* (Routledge, 2000) p.23.

6. This meant worthless or faulty – in effect, the dog had spoiled the butter making. Gibson, Marion, *Early Modern Witches*, p.32.

7. *The Examination of certaine Wytches* in Gibson, Marion, *Early Modern Witches* p.23.
8. Why Joan was also unable to call the dog to heel is unclear. Perhaps as she was not practised in witchcraft as she had so ardently protested, she did not have the skill or power to maintain control of the familiar. It is for the reader to decide whether the Queen's Attorney was serious in his offer or instead passing comment on the credulity of those assembled before him.
9. Gibson, *The Examination of certaine Wytches* p.23.
10. Elizabeth Francis was found guilty of bewitching the infant son of William Auger so that he became paralysed. Cockburn, J.S. (ed) *Calendar of Assize Records: Essex Indictments Elizabeth I* (London, 1978) p.48.
11. The full indictment against Agnes can be found in the Calendar of Assize Records for Essex. *Waterhouse, Agnes, of Hatfield Peverel, widow, indicted for murder by witchcraft. On 1st October 1565 she bewitched William Fynee at Hatfield Peverel, so that he lingered until 1 November and then died. Confessed; to hang.* Cockburn, J.S *Calendar of Assize Records: Essex Indictments Elizabeth I* (London, 1978) p.48.
12. Gibson, *The Examination of certaine Wytches* p.24.
13. *Ibid* p.24.
14. Elizabeth Francis' luck was not indefinite however, and in 1579 she also went to the gallows after a number of repeat offences.
15. There is some speculation as to whether Joan may have been a step-daughter from a previous marriage of the deceased and otherwise unknown Mr. Waterhouse. Joan's age is given as 18, which, if Agnes' age is reliably given as 64, would mean she gave birth at the age of 46, considered advanced even in the present day and age, though not impossible. (Jane Conway of Conwy for example gave birth to the last of her many children at the age of 49.) There is no indication that Agnes had any other surviving children, either of her own or her husband's, and no other family members are mentioned in the sources for her case.
16. By comparison, other names given to cat familiars were for example Puss, Jenny and Jack. Serpell, *Guardian Spirits or Demonic Pets* p.175.
17. Walker-Meikle, *Medieval Pets* p.13.
18. Maxwell-Stuart *The British Witch* p.199.
19. Briggs, *Witches and Neighbours* p.30.
20. Serpell, *Guardian Spirits or Demonic Pets* pp. 177–8.
21. The cat or the spirit inside it, had accosted her while she was on her visit to nearby Great Braxted and warned her that in the near future she would be either burned or hanged. Gibson, *The Examination of certaine Wytches* p.19.
22. The offer of the attorney to set her free if the dog could be produced could be seen as scepticism on his part, but that only meant he was unsure in this

particular instance, not denying the existence of such creatures or the Devil in general.

23. Gibson, *The Examination of certaine Wytches* p.19.
24. Stone, Lawrence *Uncertain Unions and Broken Lives* (Oxford, 1995) p.37.
25. Fletcher Anthony *Gender, Sex and Subordination in England, 1500–1800* (Yale University 1999) p.192.
26. Crawford, Patricia and Mendelson Sara, *Women in Early Modern England* (Oxford 1998) p.128.
27. It was not until 1857 that divorce as we know it came into existence, with the option for both parties to remarry. Stone, *Uncertain Unions* p.35.
28. That Agnes was not charged with Petty Treason (nor executed by burning as was the punishment for that crime) highlights that it was the death of William Fynee rather than the confession of responsibility for her husband's death that brought about her conviction.
29. Crawford and Mendelson, *Women in Early Modern England*, p.281.
30. *Ibid* p.282.
31. *Ibid* p.174.

   By her husband's death, Agnes would have achieved a certain degree of independence that she would not have known before. For example, only single and widowed women were able to own freehold land. This is unlikely to have helped Agnes in her impoverished situation. Laurence, Anne *Women in England 1500–1760* (Phoenix Press, 2002) p.229.
32. The installation can be found at the Brooklyn Museum in New York, and has been on permanent display since 2007. It consists of thirty-nine place settings set for a series of women, both historical and mythical. The goal was to redress the imbalance that led to women being left out of the historical record. Agnes' name can be found around the place setting for Petronilla de Meath, Alice Kyteler's unfortunate maid, along with Agnes Sampson, a Scottish healer executed in 1591 at the North Berwick Witch Trials, Alice Samuel, executed in 1593 and Anna Maria Schwagel, who for a long time was believed to be the last person executed for witchcraft. (It seems, however, that she actually died in prison). Angele de le Barthe, a French noblewoman who is said to have been tortured and burned alive, Anne Redferne, one of the infamous Pendle Witches who were executed in 1612. Tituba who was among the earliest to be accused of witchcraft during the Salem Witch Trials. She survived, but only after implicating others to save herself. Ursley Kemp, accused in the early part of the sixteenth century of causing the death of three people – she was executed for witchcraft. There are 999 women commemorated in the installation in total.

Chapter 3

 1. Suggett, Richard *A History of Magic and Witchcraft in Wales* (The History Press 2008) p.29.

2. It is quite clear that there was not a "witch hunt" of any sort in Wales. Improving upon the details compiled by C. L'Estrange Ewen, Richard Suggett added to the initial estimated number over twenty cases, bringing the total to thirty-four cases involving the prosecution of witchcraft between 1568 and 1699. Compared with the figures for England for the same period the number is strikingly low.

3. *Ibid* p.301. As highlighted by Sally Parkin, the Welsh did not follow the principles set out in the English Witchcraft Acts. Welsh law pre-1536 focused on ensuring the victim was compensated rather than punishing the offender, in direct contrast to the English approach to witchcraft where punishment was more prevalent. Financial compensation and the swearing of oaths in order to provide the assurance that the perpetrator would not repeat the offence were paramount.

4. Thomas, Keith *Religion and the Decline of Magic* p.589.

5. The two women who visited her were unknown to Gwen prior to this point, and there is no clue as to their identity in the documents relating to Gwen's case.

6. A hoop was a grain measurement used at the time. Another term for the same measurement was a peccaid or peck. In Montgomeryshire it measured as five gallons. A quarter bushel was called a hoop or peck in Shropshire in 1819. Zupko, Ronald Edward, *Dictionary of Weights and Measures for the British Isles: The Middle Ages To the Twentieth Century* (American Philosophical Society, 1985) p.189.

7. It is intriguing that the matter of the charm at Gloddaith, the original reason for Gwen's arrest, seems to have been forgotten by this point, as the indictments against her are utterly unrelated to the initial issue. The indictments against Gwen can be found in document *NLW Great Sessions 4/9/4 56*.

8. The exact date and place of Gwen's execution remain unknown, although it is likely that it took place not long after she was found guilty, executions tended to take place within days of the verdict being reached.

9. Suggett, Richard, *A History of Magic and Witchcraft in Wales*, p.39.

10. Suggett, Richard *Witchcraft in Early Modern Wales* in Women and Gender in Early Modern Wales ed. Roberts Michael and Clarke Simone (Cardiff 2000) p. 77. Suggett also points out that this marks a huge contrast between England and Wales with the latter displaying relatively low levels of accusations (even when slander statistics are taken into consideration) and also the lateness in the period in which they took place. The difference is all the more noteworthy as, after the Acts of Union of 1536 and 1542, Wales and England shared the same "administrative machinery." *Ibid* p.80.

11. *Ibid* p.86.

12. Serpell, James, *Guardian Spirits or Demonic Pets: The Concept of the Witch's Familiar in Early Modern England, 1530–1712* p.168.

13. Other aspects that were common to English and Continental cases but did not tend to occur in Welsh witchcraft cases were teats, paps or the Devil's mark; neither did the witches attend Sabbats or have the power to shapeshift. Parkin, Sally, *Witchcraft, Women's Honour and Customary Law in Early Modern Wales* p.299.

14. *Ibid.* p.299.

15. Suspected witches in Wales tended, on the whole, not to be from the poorest ranks of society but from the lower-middle classes. *Ibid* p.298.

16. Caerhun was fifteen miles from Gwen's home of Betws. Suggett, Richard, *A History of Magic and Witchcraft*, p.28.

17. This decidedly un-Christian feature is repeated again and again in cases of witchcraft, used as a justification for not only the witch's behaviour and giving a reason for them to act against their enemies, but also to explain and justify the actions of others against them in retaliation.

18. Maxwell-Stuart, P.G. *The British Witch*, p.165 The quickly repealed 1542 witchcraft act was actually aimed against theft magic, love magic and treasure hunting, rather than witches and, again, in 1563 it can be argued that cunning folk and learned occultists were the actual targets. Davies, Owen, *Popular Magic: Cunning Folk in English History* (Continuum 2007) pp.4–6.

19. Maxwell-Stuart, *The British Witch*, p.165 One reason for the low prosecution figures for Wales might be that there was a difficulty in demonstrating and proving an association with the Devil. Suggett, *A History of Magic*, p.64.

20. In the case of Lewis ap John for instance Gwen is reported to have told his desperate mother that she could have helped, if only the matter had not been left too late. It was the timing of things that caused the problem, not Gwen's lack of ability.

21. Parkin, *Witchcraft, Women's Honour and Customary Law in Early Modern Wales* pp.307–8.

22. The origin of the word witch in welsh is interesting as it is not a word native to Wales and was borrowed from the English. The first known example in print was in 1547, and this was used in the sense of a woman diviner or soothsayer. Gwraig/gwarch was used to refer to an ugly old woman or crone, hag, witch or sorceress, i.e. the stereotypical witch. *Ibid.* p.296.

23. Thomas, p.36.

24. *Ibid* p.34.

25. *Ibid* p.43.

26. *Ibid.* p.34.

27. Not a lot of written charms survive for Gwen's period. The best examples are from the eighteenth and nineteenth centuries. It is clear that many of these draw on earlier examples, especially those cited in Reginald Scot's *Discoverie* of 1584. Davies, Owen, *Popular Magic*, pp. 147–8.

28. Suggett, *A History of Magic and Witchcraft in Wales* p.29. Translated by Richard Suggett and reproduced with kind permission here. Although events took place in Wales, the documents regarding the case (apart from a copy of this charm that Gwen recited) are in English.
29. Thomas p.34 and *The Works of Joseph Hall*, ed. P. Wynter (Oxford 1863) vol II p.329. A popular practice was that after the practice of carrying a small candle came to an end, the use of the gospel as a charm continued and it was 'printed in a small roundel and sold to the credulous ignorants with this fond warrant, that whosoever carries it about with him shall be free from the dangers of the sayer's mishaps.' Hall 1574–1656.
30. Davies, *Popular Magic* p.149.
31. What the reason was for the change of mind is unknown. Richard Suggett suggests that the jury may well have been persuaded or coerced into changing their mind on this vital matter, pointing out that a reluctance to convict was understandable as being found guilty or not on the matter of causing death was the difference between life and death for Gwen.
32. It is perhaps worth noting in this context that St John's Gospel, which featured in this case, was said to be particularly effective as protection against thieves. Davies, Owen, *Popular Magic,* p.148.
33. The Holland family motto, ironically, was 'Let there be peace, let justice be done.' something that was not to be extended to Jane Conway's former friend Gwen.
34. Carr, A. D, *The Mostyns of Mostyn 1540–1642* Flintshire Historical Society Journal Volume 28 1977–1978 p.125.
35. Suggett, Richard, *A History of Magic and Witchcraft* p.126 In the possession of the Mostyn family from at least the fifteenth century, today, Gloddaith forms part of St David's college and despite considerable remodelling some of the sixteenth century structure still remains.
36. Although a member of the ruling class was involved, this shouldn't be interpreted in class or status terms as we would understand it today rather a case of someone with the social 'clout' to vent displeasure on another who did not. Gwen's downfall came due to her involvement in the dispute between Jane and Thomas Mostyn, in which she became entangled. Maxwell-Stuart, *The British Witch*, pp. 164–5.
37. Hughes was involved in the process of the Welsh translation of the bible, and advocated Welsh speaking priests. He was not without smear however, and he himself became subject to an inquiry – among other things, he was charged with extorting money from his own clergy during visitations.
38. Parkin, p.307.
39. Richard Suggett also reaches this conclusion, pointing out that if she had simply been carrying out her work as a healer and charmer amongst her neighbours then she would likely have remained undisturbed and unhindered

by the authorities unless someone directly brought a complaint against her. It is of note that it was only with the mention of her name in connection with the charm at Gloddaith that others came forward to accuse her of previous malefice, and even then only when invited.

Chapter 4

1. The pamphlet account of the case, *Witches Apprehended*, records that among other things cattle had miscarried and caught various diseases that had them behaving in a staggering, frenzied manner for some time. While this could be, and probably was, initially explained away as natural, newly seen in the light of what was to come they took on a whole new sinister meaning.
2. The pamphlet refers throughout to Master Enger. There is no family of this name in the parish registers for Milton Ernest however and the man in question was actually John Inger, gent.
3. In the text, Henry is referred to as 'the bastard son of Mary Sutton' with the gleeful additional note that 'for it is to be noted, that although she was never married, yet she had three bastards.' *Witches Apprehended*, in Gibson, Marion, *Early Modern Witches*, p.268.
4. *Ibid*, p.269.
5. Davies, Owen *Witchcraft, Magic and Culture 1736–1951* (Manchester University Press, 1999) p.86.
6. *Witches Apprehended*, in Gibson, Marion, *Early Modern Witches* p.266.
7. *Ibid* p.274.
8. There was the very real possibility that the accused witch would die either of the violence inflicted upon her by her overzealous accusers or from the cold or drowning. Ruth Osborne of Tring was swum by an angry mob as late as 1751 and died from the ill-treatment she suffered.
9. Maxwell-Stuart, P.G *Witch Hunters* (Tempus, 2003) p.117.
10. James I, *Daemonologie*, (London, 1603) The text states '…so it appears that God hath appointed (for a supernatural sign of the monstrous impiety of Witches) that the water shall refuse to receive them in her bosom, that have shaken off the sacred water of Baptism, and wilfully refused the benefit thereof.' p.80.
11. Keith Thomas asserts that swimming suspected witches was in use in England by 1590. Owen Davies however disagrees with this, saying that there is no evidence to support Thomas' claim. He states that although it was known to members of the educated elite, it was thus far only being used in practice on the Continent.
12. Kerr, Margaret H, *Cold Water and Hot Iron: Trial by Ordeal in England*, Richard D. Forsyth and Michael J. Plyley *The Journal of Interdisciplinary History* Vol. 22, No. 4 (Spring, 1992) p.573.
13. The earlier practice of the cucking stool dates back to the thirteenth and fourteenth centuries, and there is some evidence that the cucking stool was sometimes immersed in water. Again as with the ducking stool it was a

punishment rather than a means of establishing guilt or innocence. Both men and women could be punished in this way.

14. Cotta, John *A Short Discoverie of the Unobserved Dangers* (London 1612) p.54 In the same section he also said that he did not think that gathering to burn bewitched cattle or the burning of dung or urine of those suspected to be bewitched would bring the witch out into the open.

15. As highlighted by Owen Davies, it was truly ironic that the practice that had been introduced by the King himself and encouraged by the elite was to take so long to combat and remove from popular practices. Davies, Owen, *Witchcraft, Magic and Culture* p.90.

16. Bedfordshire and Luton Archives Service, *The Parish Register for Milton Ernest 1538–1812.*

17. As the records for the parish begin forty years before this date, one would expect there to have been some trace of either family during this time if they had lived there at this point and it can therefore be fairly assumed that they were not there before the baptisms of 1578. In that year, Robert Sutton baptised both his own son, Robert and George Sutton's son Francis.

18. In 1584 the villagers also informed against him to a visiting bishop, alleging that he not only quarrelled with his neighbours, but also that he frequented the local alehouse at unlawful times of the night. Newman, David, *The Importance of Milton Ernest* (Cromwell Press, 2006) p.13.

19. What happened to the rest of the Sutton family after Mary and her mother were executed is unclear. At the time of Mary's arrest and execution, her son George would have been 16 and Margaret around 9 years of age – Henry's age was probably between these two.

20. Their eldest daughter, Elizabeth had a son named Thomas in 1779, the father is unrecorded.

21. *The Parish Register for Milton Ernest 1538–1812* The baptism register records Mary's children as George Sutton, father unknown, baptised in 1596, and Margaret Sutton illegitimate but reputed child of Richard Page, baptised in 1604. There are very few Pages recorded for Milton Ernest, and none of the name Rich or Richard. Richard Pages baptised in Oakley in 1580, Dunton, 1577 and Stotfold, 1572 are potential candidates. There is no recorded baptism for Henry who was throwing rubbish into the mill dam where his mother was eventually tried. As expected, there is no marriage record for Mary Sutton.

22. Newman, David *The Importance of Milton Ernest* p.13.

23. *The Parish Register for Milton Ernest 1538–1812.* John, Master Inger himself was baptised in Wootton by Bedford in 1562.

24. This is unlikely to have been the son that Mary was accused of harming as the age of that child is given as seven in the pamphlet account. John on the other hand would have been just over twenty at the time and is unlikely therefore to have been the son in question.

25. Gibson, Marion, ed, *Witchcraft and Society in England and America, 1550–1750* (Cornell University Press, 2003) p.6.

Chapter 5
1. Borman, Tracy *Witches: A Tale of Sorcery, Scandal and Seduction*, (Random House. 2013) p.64.
2. Henry Manners was buried at St. Mary the Virgin, Bottesford on 26 September, 1613. Mortensen, Jennifer, *Bottesford Parish Register Transcripts*.
3. A well-established trial for proving guilt or otherwise was for the accused to eat some bread. If it was consumed without difficulty then the person was innocent, but if choking occurred it pointed firmly to guilt.
4. Unlike his brother, Francis was not buried at Bottesford but at Westminster Abbey. His mother, the Countess, was also buried there on her death in 1653.
5. *Two Sermons, Lately preached at Langar in the Valley of Belvoir* was printed in pamphlet form in 1620.
6. *The Wonderful Discovery of the Witchcrafts of Margaret and Phillip Flower*, (London, 1619) C2.
7. Mortensen, Jennifer, *Bottesford Parish Register Transcripts*.
8. Registers held at Nottinghamshire Archives.
9. HMC, *The Manuscripts of His Grace the Duke of Rutland, Preserved at Belvoir Castle, Vol IV*, (1905) p.385.
10. *Ibid* p.452, p.505.
11. Mistress tended to mean head of or lady of the house, whereas a goodwife was the term for someone of a decidedly lower status. Borman, Tracy, *Witches: A Tale of Sorcery, Scandal and Seduction* p.65.
12. Borman, Tracy, *Witches* p.65 John Flower married Helen Fenron in 1560, but, for whatever reason, the marriage doesn't seem to have been successful, as Helen married again a few years later to Lancelot Rowlston in 1564. It is possible therefore that John also remarried, and that Joan might have been his second wife.
13. *The Wonderful Discovery of the Witchcrafts of Margaret and Phillip Flower.* C3.
14. The identity of the Peake with whom Joan quarrelled and against whom the Earl refused to take her side is also worthy of note. It is possible that the man in question was actually Robert Peake the famed painter, who was not only picture maker to the elder son of James I but, after the death of the Prince, became Serjeant-Painter to the king himself. There are several references in the Rutland papers to Peake. Although there is often some confusion regarding his date of death, Peake died in 1619, the same year as Joan Flower and her daughters. One might suggest perhaps that Joan had the last laugh after all. The name is mentioned as both Peate and Peake, but there is no record of a Peate family or variant in Bottesford at the time and therefore more likely to be a member of the Peake family.

15. HMC, *Rutland*, Vol IV p.514.
16. This information regarding the meeting was related on 17th March, nearly a week after Margaret and Philippa Flower were executed.
17. Oxford English Dictionary Online, www.oed.com.
18. Snell, F. J, *The Customs of Old England*, (Reprint, 2015) p.55.
19. Thompson, Richard *Illustrations of the History of Great Britain Volume I* (Edinburgh 1828) p.166.
20. The ballad is introduced as '*Of three Lincolnshire Witches, Joan Flower, and her two daughters, Margaret and Phillip Flower, against Henry Lord Rosse, with others the Children of the Right Honourable the Earl of Rutland, at Beaver Castle, who for the same were executed at Lincoln the 11th of March last.*' It was sung to the tune of The Ladies Fall.
21. Honeybone, Michael *Wicked Practise and Sorcerye – The Belvoir Witchcraft case of 1619*, (Baron Books, 2008) p.209 There have been at least ten known re-printings of the pamphlet. The first in 1619, the latest in the twenty-first century. There is, as would be expected, a degree of poetic license, the most striking being the reference to how the Earl was grieving for the loss of his sons – the second son, however, did not die until after the pamphlet was published.
22. Throsby, John, The Supplementary Volume to the Leicestershire Views: Containing a Series of Excursions in the Year 1790, to the Villages and Places of Note in the County (1790) p.155.
23. Borman, Tracy, *Witches* p.193 The three women are depicted in a woodcut illustration attached to the pamphlet account of Joan and her daughters – known to be local cunning women, Joan Wilimot and Anne Baker gave evidence that served to further prove the guilt of Joan and her daughters. Anne Baker was said by those in the area to have been responsible for the murder of two local children through her witchcraft, a fact she denied.
24. Gibson, Marion, *Early Modern Witches* p.298.
25. Borman, *Witches* pp.201–2.
26. The greatly unpopular Buckingham was stabbed to death at the Greyhound Pub in Portsmouth on 23 August – his assassin was an army officer named John Felton with several grievances against the Duke.
27. Thomas, *Religion and the Decline of Magic*, p.519.
28. Stone, Lawrence, *Uncertain Unions and Broken Lives* (Oxford 1995) pp. 46, 72.
29. Honeybone, *Wicked Practise and Sorcerye* p.53.
30. HMC, *Rutland*, Vol IV p.516.
31. Thomas, p.277.
32. *Ibid* p.519.
33. There are buildings dating from the relevant period still remaining in Bottesford, but these are the parish church and two almshouses, the Earl of Rutland's Hospital, and Dr Fleming's Hospital. Although the foundations of

the cottage in question may date from the seventeenth century, this does not in itself prove a connection to Joan and her family.

34. One of the most noted was the 'Leicester Artist' John Flower, known for his landscapes and architectural paintings.

35. Published in 1956, it was one of Lewis' popular historical novels, and although some creative liberties are taken, it makes for a gripping read. Although a great deal of Lewis' works are now out of print, *The Witch and the Priest* has been re-issued by Valancourt Books.

36. Honeybone, p.198.

37. Due to her status as an accused witch, it has been suggested that Joan was not granted burial in the churchyard and was therefore probably buried in unconsecrated ground, either outside the churchyard or elsewhere.

Chapter 6

1. The idea that witches were burned was firmly established in England by the middle of the seventeenth century, even though nearly every witch condemned from 1563 onwards had been hanged. Gaskill, Malcolm, *Witchfinders A Seventeenth-Century English Tragedy* (John Murray Publishers 2006) p.173 The last heretic to be burned in England was Edward Wightman from Burton-on-Trent, executed in 1612 at Lichfield.

2. In The History and Antiquities of the Flourishing Corporation of Kings Lynn, published by Benjamin Mackerell in 1738 it is recorded that Margaret Read was burnt at Kings Lynn for witchcraft in 1590. Mother Green's fiery death at Pocklington in 1630 also made it into the parish registers for the town, where it was remarked that 'Old wife Green burnt in Market for a witch.' Two mentions of burnings are made in Browne's History of Norwich, where 'Two old women, (one of whom, named Tirrel, belonged to the hospital) were burnt on a charge of witchcraft.' There is little to nothing of further supporting evidence for these cases however.

3. *The Lawes against Witches and Conjuration and Some brief Notes and Observations for the Discovery of Witches* (1645).

4. No further information is given regarding this or the sort of magic Mary employed to carry out her revenge on those she disliked other than the sending of the spirit. The methods used by witches would have been well known to the audience reading the pamphlet and the author either did not have the details or did not feel the need to elaborate as the rest spoke for itself.

5. The medieval structure was located next to the west gate and conditions were likely to have been decidedly grim for those held there. Jones, David L, *The Ipswich Witch: Mary Lackland and the Suffolk Witch Hunts* (The History Press 2015) p.11.

6. SROB C8/4/7, *Sessions of the Peace, Borough of Ipswich* 1645.

7. Gaskill, *Witchfinders*, p.176.

8. Alice Denham, another Ipswich widow, was found guilty of felony and witchcraft and for feeding imps. On 12 July 1645 four men were paid £10 for giving evidence against her. She pleaded not guilty on the charges against her but was convicted. SROB C8/4/7, *Sessions of the Peace, Borough of Ipswich* 1645.

9. *The Witch of Wapping or an Exact and Perfect Relation of the Life and Devilish Practices of Joan Peterson* (1652) p.8.

10. Redstone's *Memorials of Old Suffolk* asserts that she was probably over 70 years of age at the time of her trial, but it is unclear what this is based upon, whilst Malcolm Gaskill puts Mary's age at closer to 50.

11. Jones, *The Ipswich Witch*, p.180.

12. McCurrach, M, *Freemen of the Borough of Ipswich part Two* (Suffolk Family History Society, 2000) pp.2–3.

13. John and Mary's son George however acquired his freeman status by patrimony, that is he had to be at least 21, born in wedlock, and with a father who was a freeman. Purchase and presentation were the other two options available to someone wanting to become a freeman. McCurrach, M, *Freemen of the Borough of Ipswich part Two* (Suffolk Family History Society, 2000) pp.2–3.

14. He had four children, John, Susanna, Mary and Abigail, all born in the 1620s.

15. Defoe, Daniel *The Political History of the Devil* (London, 1727) p.356.

16. Wodderspoon, John, *A New Guide to Ipswich* p.83.

17. Cabell Craig, *Witchfinder General: The Biography of Matthew Hopkins* (The History Press, 2006) p.58.

18. 'As she confessed' is added after each point on which Mary was accused and the account is titled as a confession, both of which are misleading when other evidence is considered.

19. Even if she had been convinced to confess at the end, that does not mean she necessarily considered herself to be guilty of what she was accused. Although torture was forbidden by law, there were less "official" methods of getting the accused to speak. Sleep deprivation was one method that proved most effective; a woman from Hoxne, near Norfolk, confessed to all manner of things, including having a familiar named Nan, only to wake after finally being allowed a night's sleep to remember nothing of the affair at all. It later transpired that she had a hen that she used to call by that name.

20. SROB C8/4/7, *Sessions of the Peace, Borough of Ipswich* 1645.

21. *The Lawes against Witches and Conjuration and Some brief Notes and Observations for the Discovery of Witches* (1645).

22. This particular part of the act, which is still in force in a greatly amended form today, was only abolished in 1828.

23. Crawford and Mendelson, *Women in Early Modern England*, p.44.

24. Laurence, Anne *Women in England 1500–1760 A Social History* (Phoenix 1996) p.269.

25. Crawford and Mendelson, p.44 Ipswich was also no stranger to burnings, in the not too distant past, two women, Anne Potter, a brewer's wife, and Joan Trunchfield, a shoemaker's wife, were recorded as apprehended and imprisoned, and were both burnt at Ipswich, February 19, 1556.

26. In contrast to the number of trials, it was reported that thirty-eight suspected witches were imprisoned over the summer of 1645. *The True Informer*, 23 July 1645.

27. Jones, p.30.

28. It has been suggested that although it cost the town a great deal to execute Mary Lakeland, it also cost a considerable amount to keep a minimum of 300 needy poor supported for years, and that killing Mary was therefore ultimately cheaper than keeping her. Jones, p.175.

29. Gaskill, *Witchfinders*, p.178.

30. *Ibid* pp.177, 312.

31. *SROB C8/4/7, Sessions of the Peace, Borough of Ipswich 1645.*

32. In addition to this rigorous routine there were also church services on Sundays and another three hour lecture at the church of St. Mary Tower. Jones, pp.24–5.

33. *Ibid*, p.182.

34. Gaskill, *Witchfinders*, p.174.

35. Jones, p.183.

36. Clarke, G. R, *The History and Description of the Town and Borough of Ipswich* p.342.

37. Deacon, Richard *Matthew Hopkins Witch Finder General* (Anchor Press 1976) p.158.

38. *Ibid.*, p.158.

39. *The Tendring Witchcraft Revelations* upon which Deacon claims to have based his work was, according to a note in the text, 'the title of an unpublished manuscript by C. S Perryman, dated 1725, which incorporates material compiled by 'divers informers' in 1645, 1646, 1647 and 1648–50." He even goes so far as to add a mention in the acknowledgements to the book: 'to Miss Victoria Empson for permission to inspect and make quotations from the *Tendring Witchcraft Revelations* Papers and for assistance in deciphering some of this manuscript.' Richard Deacon had form when it comes to this sort of fabrication. Under the pen name of Donald McCormick, he wrote several books on controversial subjects based on 'secret' sources that were in truth made up by him entirely. For an in-depth look at his many fabrications, see *Friedrich Hayek: A Collaborative Biography Part III, Fraud, Fascism and Free Market Religion*, Leeson, Robert (Ed.), (Palgrave Macmillan, 2015).

40. Cabell, Craig, *Witchfinder General*, p.56–8.

41. Jones, p.16.

42. Gaskill, *Witchfinders*, p.177.

43. *Ibid* p. xiii.

44. Worden, Blair, *The English Civil Wars* 1640–1660, (W&N, 2010) p.1.
45. Maxwell-Stuart, *The British Witch*, p.241.
46. *Ibid* p.433, Note 52.
47. *The Lawes against Witches and Conjuration and Some brief Notes and Observations for the Discovery of Witches* (1645).
48. *Ibid* p.6.
49. Gaskill *Witchfinders*, p.47 The Protestation Oath, whereby all those over the age of 18 were to swear allegiance to King Charles I and the Church of England, and the Solemn League and Covenant in particular were at the forefront of people's minds.
50. Ewen, C. L'Estrange, *Witchcraft and Demonism*, (1933) p.62.
51. Puttick, *Betty Ghosts of Suffolk* (Bristol, 2004) pp.13–15 The tale of Mary's lingering presence is also covered in Pete Jennings' *Supernatural Ipswich*.

Chapter 7

1. Stone, Brian, *Derbyshire in the Civil War*, (Scarthin Books, 1992) Introduction.
2. *Ibid.* p.94. This level of trauma and destruction on a social level was greater than even the First World War so it comes as little surprise that the people of Derbyshire opted out of the Second Civil War which was ended by the execution of Charles I on 30 January 1649.
3. Although the Toleration Act of September 1650 repealed the law on compulsory attendance at church, there were several pieces of legislation that were less accommodating. Several pieces of legislation came into being the following year, among them the Adultery Act which though never applied in practice, gave the death penalty for adultery and fornication, and the blasphemy Act of August that year to tackle 'religious enthusiasm.'
4. The concept of being witch or hag ridden was not uncommon in witchcraft accusations and was used to explain what is now referred to as sleep paralysis. Symptoms include being unable to move or talk and usually occurs in the moments before waking, or just after falling asleep. The experience can be very unsettling and cause great distress.
5. Q/SB/2/170. The church as it is today is unrecognisable from how it would have been in Anne's time. The graves from the seventeenth century are non existent, and it is possible that her burial was unmarked if feeling against her and the family was still negative, the association of witchcraft still present. It was not, however, enough to have chased her from the area.
6. Quarter Sessions were courts held, as the name implies, four times a year. They were chaired by two Justices and a jury, and dealt with cases that could not be dealt with by the Petty Sessions. They also decided which cases were to be sent on to the Assizes. Quarter Sessions ceased to be held in 1972 when they were replaced by the modern Crown Court system we know today.

7. Ewen, C. L'Estrange, ed, *Witch Hunting and Witch Trials* (London, 1929) pp.52–53. A person suspecting another of committing a felony – which in this time, witchcraft was – were within their rights to take that person to a justice or constable and voice their suspicions. At this point, 'Information' would be taken from those who accused the person and the supporting witnesses. The suspected witch could be taken into custody or could still be free at this point, but once the information had been laid, the magistrate would then set about an enquiry. The information of witnesses and the original informants were written down and both were bound over to appear before the next courts.

8. Survival of assize records for Derbyshire are incredibly poor, existing only from 1932. There is therefore no knowing for certain whether Anne actually faced trial there.

9. Flinders, Stephen and Heather, ed. *Ilkeston St Mary's The Parish Registers 1588–1699.*

10. *Ilkeston Manor Court Rolls*, Waterhouse MSS 50a, Ilkeston Local Studies Library.

11. Trueman, Edwin, *History of Ilkeston*, (John F. Walker, 1880) p.156.

12. *Ibid.* p.155.

13. Notestein, Wallace *A History of Witchcraft in England from 1558–1718* (Lord Baltimore Press, 1911) p.219.

14. Flinders, Stephen and Heather, ed. *Ilkeston St Mary's The Parish Registers 1588–1699.*

15. *Ibid.*

16. *Ibid.*

17. Flinders, Stephen *Ilkeston Families of the 16th and 17th Centuries.* Volume I (2007) p.1 Due to a judicious amount of intermarrying, by the time of Anne's case the prominent families of the area were all connected to each other. By 1600 there were one hundred male and female copyholders and tenants in Ilkeston, amongst which the names of Harvey, Hellot, Day and Webster are included.

18. Flinders, Stephen and Heather, ed. *Ilkeston St Mary's The Parish Registers 1588–1699.*

19. *Ibid.*

20. This concept had long existed. It was also more than just a superstition held by the lower orders, the possibility of oscular fascination was upheld in Oxford in 1600. Thomas, p.50.

21. Hutton, William *The History of Derby* (London, 1817) p.84. Davies, R. T *Four Centuries of Witch Beliefs* (Routledge, 2011) pp.165–6.

22. *Ibid.* p.167.

23. Trueman, *Edwin History of Ilkeston* p.22 The Committee for Plundered Ministers would hear evidence, often from local parishioners, of the errors in doctrine of the parish priest. If the allegations were proven the rector was replaced and his property forcibly sequestered, so that he could only recover it

by buying it back. Although Fox retained his living until about 1654 when he was replaced by the registrar William Harvey it may well be that he suffered from animosity in his congregation and further afield due to his 'scandalous' status.

24. *"This was Justice Bennett of Darby that first called us Quakers because wee bid ym tremble at ye Word of God and this was in ye year 1650."* Penney, Norman, ed. *The Journal of George Fox* (Cambridge University Press, 1911) p.4.

25. *Ibid* p.13.

26. Although it is not clear how or if George and William Fox were related, George Fox had a sister called Dorothy, born in 1626 and William Fox had a daughter of the same name born a decade later that suggests a potential, if tentative, connection. Hatton, Jean George Fox: *A Biography of the Founder of the Quakers* (Monarch Books, 2007) p.17 Even were there no connection, a simple dislike of the name of 'Fox' may have been enough to prejudice him against the informants from Ilkeston.

27. In 1663 the year of his mother's death, John Wagg was fined for being absent from his court duty. Interestingly a George Wagg was fined in 1665 for failing to attend the Manor Court and is listed as gent, suggesting a rise in status for the family. At the same session, John Wagg was fined for taking wood from the park without permission.

28. A short essay written on the case in the 1970s suggests that suspicion fell on Anne due to her propensity for gossip, the author helpfully going on to point out that this was a particularly female trait and to speculate whether burning might not be a general solution! A newspaper article from a local paper refers to a talk given by the senior history master at nearby Heanor Grammar school making the claim that 'Annie Wagg' was not a pleasant person, softening the blow by adding that this did not, necessarily, make her a murderer.

Chapter 8

1. Goodare, Julian; Martin, Lauren, Miller, Joyce, and Yeoman, Louise, *The Survey of Scottish Witchcraft*, http://www.shca.ed.ac.uk/witches/ (archived January 2003, accessed 20/9/2015).

2. Wilby, Emma, *The Visions of Isobel Gowdie: Magic, Witchcraft and Dark Shamanism in Seventeenth-Century Scotland.* (Sussex Academic Press, 2013) p.3.

3. Janet or Jenny was a generic term for a witch in some areas of Scotland during the seventeenth century.

4. All of these were local people who she would have seen on a regular basis: John Young, a warlock and the coven's leader; Jonet Braidheid; Margaret Brodie; and Katherine Sowter to name but a few who appear regularly throughout Isobel's confessions.

5. In Anglo-Saxon England, around the ninth century, it was considered that chickenpox, measles and smallpox were all caused by wounds from swarms of elf archers, all aspects of these diseases were known as 'elf-sickness' and could be cured by applying holy water to affected parts. Not until Rhazes' Treatise on Smallpox were the different diseases separated, and it would seem as though some of this superstition lingered in the Highlands.

6. It was easy enough for Isobel and her fellow witches to carry out this and their other excursions without being missed at home; to avoid detection Isobel told how she and her associates simply left brooms in their beds so that their husbands would not know they had gone.

7. Confession Four, in Wilby, Emma, *The Visions of Isobel Gowdie* (Sussex Academic Press, 2013) p.51.

8. Confession Three, In Wilby, Emma, *The Visions of Isobel Gowdie*, (2013) p.47.

9. Confession Three, In Wilby, Emma, *The Visions of Isobel Gowdie*, (2013) p.47.

10. Confession Two, in Wilby, Emma, *The Visions of Isobel Gowdie*, (2013) p.43.

11. *Ibid.*

12. The outcome was not initially a forgone conclusion; the majority of witchcraft accusations did not go further than the accusation stage even in Scotland. By the time she was committed to trial, however, it was likely that the outcome was certain and that a verdict of guilty was the required result.

13. Wilby, Emma, *The Visions of Isobel Gowdie*, p.34 Scottish witches, unlike English ones, were burned rather than hanged if sentenced to death.

14. Maxwell-Stuart, *The British Witch*, p.278.

15. The confessions themselves took place on 13 April, 3 May, 15 May, and 27 May 1662 and their frequency suggests that Isobel was kept confined or imprisoned throughout as there is nothing to suggest that she was set at liberty and re-apprehended each time. Whether she was allowed visitors or not is unknown, although the nature of the confessions would suggest that she was to be kept away from her 'coven' and from her neighbours.

16. Wilby, Emma *The Visions of Isobel Gowdie,* p.8.

17. *Ibid.* pp.13–14.

18. Anderson, Michael, *British Population History From the Black Death to the Present Day* (Cambridge University Press, 1996) pp.127–8.

19. Maxwell-Stuart, *The British Witch* p.278.

20. Maxwell-Stuart suggests this theory and Emma Wilby also argues that Isobel's confessions, far from the ravings of madness, were more indicative of a visionary experience.

21. A disease caused by the fungus *claviceps purpurea*, such poisoning has been used to tenuously explain several witch crazes including the convulsions experienced by alleged victims in the Salem Witch Trials.

22. Barger, George, *Ergot and Ergotism*, (1931) p.36.

23. Wilby p.127.

24. It would not after all be the last time that someone facing trial used popular culture to colour how they tell their stories and there are modern cases with apparently innocent people confessing to crimes they did not commit.

25. Pugh, Roy J. M, *The Devl's Ain* (Harlaw Heritage, 2001) p.127.

26. This explanation, whilst not only being the least viable based on the evidence (there is no evidence to suggest either way regarding Isobel's personality) does much to illuminate the often still misogynistic beliefs regarding women accused of witchcraft today.

27. Goodare, Julian, *Women and the Witch Hunt in Scotland, Social History*. Vol. 23, No. 3 (Oct., 1998) p.290.

28. Maxwell-Stuart, *The British Witch*, pp. 278–9.

29. The main exponent of this idea, Margaret Murray, agrees that the origin of the word is to convene, but argues that it was a band or company 'set apart for the practice of the rites of the religion and for the performance of magical ceremonies; in short, a kind of priesthood.' Her book, *The Witch Cult in Western Europe* has been highly influential in spreading this idea. The evidence she uses however is strongly suspect, and as highlighted by Keith Thomas, it has been twisted to fit her theory and used confessions that were probably procured under torture. Thomas, Keith p.615.

30. Goodare, Julian, Martin, Lauren, Miller, Joyce, and Yeoman, Louise, *The Survey of Scottish Witchcraft*, http://www.shca.ed.ac.uk/witches/ (archived January 2003, accessed 20/9/2015).

31. Maxwell-Stuart *The British Witch* p.278.

32. Although decidedly fantastical these claims were not unique. There was a case prior to Isobel's in March of 1662. Marie or Mary Lamont made the surprising offer to be tried, citing God's direction to confess as her reason for doing so. She accordingly told how she had first renounced her baptism, before handing herself over to the Devil. She did this by placing one hand on her head and the other on the bottom of her foot, before saying she gave everything that was in-between to her new master. Pugh, Roy, *The Deil's Ain*, p.125.

33. Goodare, Julian, Martin, Lauren, Miller, Joyce, and Yeoman, Louise, *The Survey of Scottish Witchcraft*, http://www.shca.ed.ac.uk/witches/ (archived January 2003, accessed 20/9/2015).

34. Cowan, Edward J and Henderson, Lizanne, *Scottish Fairy Belief A History* (2001) p.41,

35. The Reverend Robert Kirk had a life-long fascination for everything to do with fairies and authored the well-known and influential *The Secret Commonwealth*. After his death in 1692 rumours and legends arose that Kirk had been taken to fairyland for good as he had shared too many of the secrets of that world. *The Secret Commonwealth* was not published until 1815.

36. Wilby, p.31,

37. Isobel's third confession. Wilby, p.49.

38. Composer's Notes, *The Confession of Isobel Gowdie* (1990) (c) Copyright by James MacMillan.

Chapter 9

1. In 1717, Jane Clarke along with her daughter and son were accused of causing illness and misery through bewitchment in Great Wigston, Leicestershire. Twenty-five of their neighbours felt strongly enough to speak against them, although the case was eventually thrown out and the Clarke's were not convicted.
2. Bragge, Francis, *A Full and Impartial Account of the Discovery of Sorcery and Witchcraft, Practis'd by Jane Wenham of Walkern*, (London, 1712) p.2.
3. *Ibid* p.7.
4. *Ibid*. p.10.
5. *Ibid*. p.16.
6. *Ibid* p.19.
7. *Ibid*.
8. *Ibid*. p.21.
9. *Ibid* p.24.
10. *Ibid* p.22.
11. *Ibid*. p.29.
12. *Ibid*. p.35.
13. Hutchinson, Francis *An Historical Essay Concerning Witchcraft* (London 1718) p.130.
14. D/EP/F234, Sarah Cowper's Day Book, 16 – 17 Dec 1729, Hertfordshire Archives and Local Studies.
15. Francis Bragge is also often confused with the Mr Bragge who is mentioned as being present at the Gardiner's house when Anne Thorn first fell ill in the kitchen, with the two men claimed to be one and the same. Mr Bragge however was Francis Bragge's father. Francis Bragge Senior was vicar of Hitchin, and had married Jane Chauncy, the daughter of Henry Chauncy, who also played a prominent role in Jane's case.
16. Bragge, *Full and Impartial Account*, p.13.
17. *Ibid*. p.28.
18. *Ibid*. p.28.
19. Interestingly, it appears that Edward Wenham's family had fallen on hard times; his father and grandfather had been local blacksmiths, but, with his father dying when Edward was young, the smithy passed into other hands, leaving the family with decreased economic status. Guskin, Phyllis J, *The Context of Witchcraft: The Case of Jane Wenham (1712)* Eighteenth Century Studies. Vol 15, No 1 (Autumn, 1981) p.60.
20. DP/114/1/1 Burial of Phillip Cook/Cooke 1696, Walkern, Hertfordshire Archives and Local Studies.

21. DP/114/1/2 Marriage of Jane Cooke and Edward Wenham, 1697, Walkern, Hertfordshire Archives and Local Studies.
22. DP/114/1/2 Baptism December 1679, Elizabeth Cooke, Walkern, Hertfordshire Archives and Local Studies.

    DP/114/1/2 Baptism December 1681, Sarah Cooke, Walkern, Hertfordshire Archives and Local Studies.
23. Sarah Cooke had married in 1703 in Walkern to a man named George Sherwood from the parish of Baldock, whether the couple had children or what became of the Sherwoods is unknown. DP/114/1/2 Hertfordshire Archives and Local Studies.
24. Briggs, p.46.
25. Briggs, p.57.
26. *The Case of the Hertfordshire Witchcraft Consider'd* (London, 1712) p.69.
27. Bragge, Francis *Witchcraft father display'd* (London, 1712) p.iii.
28. Bragge, *Full and Impartial Account*, p.12.
28. *The Case of the Hertfordshire Witchcraft Consider'd* (London, 1712) p.78.
30. *Ibid* p.78.
31. *Ibid* p.81.
32. DP/53/1/3 Marriage of Anne Thorn and James Bonnill/Bonvill, Hertfordshire Archives and Local Studies.
33. The speculation made that she was pregnant therefore cannot be substantiated by a handy baptism record, and must remain just that – speculation. It is also worthy of note that Thomas Ireland, who also gave evidence against Jane, married Anne Street, the other girl to claim Jane had bewitched her.
34. The first performance of *Jane Wenham: The Witch of Walkern* was at Watford Palace Theatre on 23 September 2015. From there it embarked on a national tour, receiving predominantly positive reviews based upon a sterling cast and the frank exploration of witch hunts both then and now. The play was not, however, received entirely without controversy; a Suffolk girls' school cancelled a booked performance at their venue, citing that the themes explored within the play were not deemed suitable for their students. This incident is in itself a damning indictment of society's desire to ignore and thus perpetuate prejudices and taboos surrounding uncomfortable topics such as sexuality and consent.

    Amanda Bellamy makes for a deeply sympathetic, and often heart-breaking, Jane Wenham, by turns defiant and bewildered as she is isolated and tormented by her neighbours. She epitomises, as the historical Jane does throughout the sources, many well-documented attributes common to those who were accused as a witch. Unafraid to speak her mind, elderly and vulnerable due to a lack of protection from husband or family, Bellamy's Jane retains her spirit to the last, broken but not defeated as she shouts curses on the village as she is led away.

Chapter 10

1. The Act was put before the Commons on 27 January, receiving royal assent on 24 March before passing into law on 24 June. The 1604 Witchcraft Act was effectively repealed, and there was also the telling addition to the new legislation, stating that it was 'for the more effectual preventing and punishing any pretences to such arts or powers as are before mentioned, whereby ignorant persons are frequently deluded and defrauded.' Davies, Owen, *Witchcraft, Magic and Culture 1736–1951* (Manchester University Press, 1999) p.2.

2. It had been possible to bring a slander case against someone for calling one a witch in the past, but not until the 1736 Act was the law predisposed to be on the side of the accused.

3. *Exeter and Plymouth Gazette*, 24 April 1852, p.7 www.britishnewspaperarchive.co.uk.

4. *Ibid.*

5. *Ibid.*

6. Mary Pile's fine would be roughly the equivalent of £80 today, while Walter Gooding was charged £50 for the pleasure of assaulting Susannah.

7. *Taunton Courier, and Western Advertiser,* 18 July, 1860, p.2 www.britishnewspaperarchive.co.uk.

8. *Ibid.* Mr Holmes' response to this was not given in the account.

9. *Ibid.*

10. White, William, History, *Gazetteer, and Directory of Devonshire,* (Simkin, Marshall and Company, 1850) pp.225–6 Colaton Raleigh. The Colaton part of the name is said to come from being the 'tun' or farm of the chief. The Raleigh part was added when the village came into the possession of the Raleigh family in the thirteenth century.

11. *Devon Family History Society Baptism index,* 1813–1827.

12. *Colaton Raleigh Parish, Register of Marriages,* Devon Heritage Centre. Susannah's new surname was variously spelt as Sellick, Sullock and Zellek throughout the parish registers. Henry Selleck descended from Jacob and Hannah Sellick and their sons, present in the village since at least the early 1700s.

13. They were also living with 25-year-old Simon Sellick. Hawkerland was a hamlet of Colaton Raleigh. Francis Sellick, head of another branch of Henry's prolific family, lived next door.

14. 2973A/PR/1/11, *Colaton Raleigh Parish, Register of Burials,* Devon Heritage Centre. Henry Sellick's death certificate records his age as 84.

15. That the newspapers reported Susannah as being a widow is interesting in itself, the stereotype of the elderly, widowed witch no doubt perceived to make a better story.

16. *Devon family History Society Burial index,* 1813–1839.

17. At the time of the 1871 Census a decade later, this arrangement was still going strong; the 88-year-old Susannah was living with Caroline (82), and the 61-year-old Sarah in the hamlet of Hawkerland.
18. Davies, Owen, *Witchcraft, Magic and Culture 1736–1951* p.193.
19. A similar case was reported in the *Exeter and Plymouth Gazette* for 13 March, 1852. Charity Furker of Crewkerne charged Grace Webb with attacking her, drawing blood, calling her a witch and accusing her of hag riding her and also causing the death of several others by witchcraft. The girl, Charity's niece, swore to be in fear of her life. Her mother and herself were convinced of the truth of the matter and would not be swayed.

    Another case was reported in the *North Devon Journal* for 16 September, 1852 under the title 'Reputed Witchcraft' regarding the attack on Sarah Squibb at Blandford, Devon, by a jeweller named Matthais. Sarah was 'aged and decrepid' and reputed to be a witch; Matthais attacked her with a knife enough to draw blood and was fined 10s plus costs for the privilege.
20. *North Devon Journal*, 29 April, 1852, p.7 www.britishnewspaperarchive.co.uk.
21. There are several references to the use in Roman times, where a nail would be nailed into a house wall to protect against plague. This was also in evidence at the Temple of Jupiter, where they were said to be driven into the walls in an effort to protect against charms and the rising up of factions.
22. Fawrar, Janet and Stewart, *Spells and How They Work* (Robert Hale, 2010).
23. *Exeter and Plymouth Gazette,* 6 October, 1860, p.7 www.britishnewspaperarchive. co.uk.

    Drawing blood from his own mother prompted the magistrates to publicly note that it was 'rather discouraging to find such instances of gross ignorance and superstition.' *The Western Times*, 6 October, 1860 also commented on the John Bolt case by pointing out that Mary Bolt must have been suffering much to take her own son before the courts.

    John and Frances Bolt had at least seven children in the period between 1845 and the incident. In the 1861 census, John is recorded as at home with two of the children but with no sign of his wife. She is likewise absent in the 1871 census, but returns in the 1881. John Bolt had a colourful life indeed – he was called to court in 1865 by his wife Frances, making the same complaint that his mother had tried to address regarding lack of support for their family of at least seven children; he was in court again a few years later accused of kidnapping the 15-year-old daughter of his housekeeper who had lived with the family after his wife finally left him.
24. Petty sessions were the lowest rung of the judicial system, and sittings were heard before Justices or Magistrates without a jury. Put in place at the beginning of the eighteenth century in order to relieve the over-taxed Quarter Sessions, these sittings heard cases dealing with a range of undesirable behaviours, such as drunkenness, assault and minor theft.

25. 1853 saw the repeal of advertisement duty, and stamp duty was repealed in 1855, opening the floodgates where newspaper readership and advertising were concerned. After 1850 there were at least a hundred new newspapers that came into existence in neighbouring Somerset alone. Printing techniques were also improving all the time, as were methods of distribution. Davies, Owen, *A People Bewitched*,(David and Charles, 2012).
26. *Taunton Courier, and Western Advertiser,* 18 July, 1860, p.2 www.britishnewspaper archive.co.uk.
27. *Supplement to the Western Times*, Exeter, 14 July, 1860, p.3 www.britishnewspaper archive.co.uk.
28. Attitudes towards women in the newspapers of the time were varied and ranged from sympathy to outright misogyny. In the accounts dealing with witchcraft the reporting tends to be on the side of the attacked woman, the lack of reason and sense of those making the accusations being highlighted, rather than gender being the deciding factor. This is in contrast to reporting in general where, in many cases, women are not treated well.
29. There are parts of the church that go back to the twelfth and thirteenth centuries, although the church itself in general has been restyled since Susannah's time, having been remodelled in 1875.
30. This was carried out by a series of registrars and the country was divided into registration districts, based loosely on the old poor law unions. From 1 July 1837, the event had to be registered in the area in which it had taken place. The Registrar General at the General Record Office then collated them all together in a central record. It was the responsibility of the registrar to find out and register the events that took place in the district, until the law changed in 1874 and it became the responsibility of the parents, with a fine imposed if the birth were not registered within a set amount of time. This was largely to assist the new Boards of Health in tracking the incidence of disease as well as streamline tax records and provide data for the new study of demographics that would support the 1875 Public Health Act.
31. The level of detail the census returns can give are varied. In the 1841 census for example, the enumerators who collected the information from householders did not give a precise age – instead they were to round down to the nearest multiple of five. In future years this became more precise, with address, occupation and birthplace given in varying detail.
32. There is a death of a Robert Pile in 1852, the year of the incident with Susannah. It would be interesting to learn of the cause of death and whether it had any connection with the allegations against Susannah.
33. A clue as to the identity of her father is that in the 1881 census she was listed as grand-daughter to the Vinnicomes – their eldest son, Thomas, was born in 1851 and a likely candidate for paternity where Elizabeth Ebdon was concerned. Elizabeth herself married Frederick Pile at Colaton Raleigh in 1901, and Virginia lived with them until her death in 1920. In the 1911 census she is listed

as an invalid; with Susannah being long dead by that point, one would hope she was not posthumously blamed for the elderly Virginia's condition.

34. 2973A/PR/1/12, Colaton Raleigh Parish, Register of Burials, Devon Heritage Centre.

Chapter 11

1. This is the generally accepted average, although some estimates come in as much higher depending on the definition of casualty chosen.
2. Shandler, Nina, *The Strange Case of Hellish Nell* (Da Capo Press, 2006) p.18
3. Most historians of the Second World War accept that there was no Nazi spy-ring in Britain by the beginning of hostilities. All Nazi spies were already known to the authorities and fed misinformation or had been turned and were double-agents; the few who were not fled in short order.
4. 'Albert' had been working as Helen's spirit control – a guide or intermediary between the entranced medium and the spirit world – since 1928. He was said to have been a pattern maker from Dundee before he had emigrated to Australia, dying at the age of 33 or 34 from causes unknown. Tall and well spoken, Albert brooked no nonsense, and was known to disapprove of Helen's husband Henry, arguing with, and insulting, him on more than one occasion. There is to this date no proof of the historical existence of Albert Stewart.
5. Gaskill, Malcolm, *Hellish Nell Last of Britain's Witches* (Fourth Estate, 2001) p.191.
6. *Ibid.* p.192.
7. Helen had taken to wearing her 'séance outfit' when she did sittings to avoid suggestions of fraud. Comprising of black under garments, dress and shoes, this clothing was checked by independent witnesses before a sitting began so that it would be impossible for her to conceal the props and other paraphernalia associated with mediums and fraud.
8. Although several people demanded to be searched in order to prove Helen's innocence, Christine (the Homer's daughter) among them, the request was refused, an omission on the part of the authorities that has never been explained satisfactorily.
9. Gaskill, *Hellish Nell*, p.193.
10. Cassrier, Manfred, *Medium on Trial: The Story of Helen Duncan and The Witchcraft Act* (PN Publishing, 1996) p.57.
11. Davies, Owen, *Witchcraft, Magic and Culture 1736–1951*, p.2.
12. Although Helen had twelve pregnancies in total, sadly only six children lived to adulthood.
13. Cassrier, Manfred, *Medium on Trial*, p.111, Gaskill, *Hellish Nell*, p.213.
14. Davies, Owen, *Witchcraft, Magic and Culture*, p.72.
15. Maule was an Edinburgh spiritualist who invited mediums into her home to hold séances there.
16. Gaskill, *Hellish Nell*, p.154.

17. *Ibid* p.156.
18. Brealey, Gena, *The Two Worlds of Helen Duncan* (Saturday Night Press, 2008) p.102.
19. Gaskill, Malcolm, *Hellish Nell*, p.194.
20. Shandler, Nina *The Strange Case of Hellish Nell*, (Da Capo Press, 2006) pp.41–2.
21. Ibid p.80.
22. *The Barham Conspiracy*, in World War II Magazine, December 2004. The pretence was so complete that Christmas and New Year cards were sent to families in the names of those who perished.
23. Price noted that all other orifices and potential places of concealment had been examined by trained medical staff without evidence of cheesecloth, and that therefore, the only possible explanation for Helen's materialisations must be that she was regurgitating cheesecloth at will.
24. The pictures taken can be found freely on the internet today, and also in Price's book.
25. Price, Harry, *Leaves from a Psychist's Case-Book (Victor Gollancz, 1933)* p.204.
26. *Ibid* p.201.
27. Cassrier, Manfred, *Medium on Trial* (P N Publishing, 1996) p.149.
28. *Ibid* p.154.
29. Allegations of this nature were not unique to Helen by any means; famous mediums Eva Carrière and Eusapia Palladino among others had known similar charges and had at various points been discovered in fraud.
30. Cassrier, *Medium on Trial*, p.152.
31. Price, Harry, *Leaves from a Psychist's Case-Book*, pp. 207–8.
32. Roberts, C.E. Bechhofer, *The Trial of Mrs Duncan*, (Jarrolds, 1945) p.171.
33. The couple were later married, with, it appears, the blessing of the deceased Mrs Woodcock.
34. Cassrier, p.78.
35. These and further testimonies can be found in the most complete account of Helen's trial, *The Trial of Mrs Duncan* edited by C.E. Bechhofer Roberts.
36. Shandler, p.3.
37. Cassrier, p.151.
38. Davies, Owen *Witchcraft, Magic and Culture*, p.73.
39. Under the new Act displays of psychic powers that were carried out for the purpose of entertainment were safe, and thus those performing them were not liable to prosecution.
40. Gaskill, *Hellish Nell*, pp.360–362.

Afterword
1. The 72-year-old London-based medium was arrested on claims that she was playing on wartime fears to exploit and defraud a vulnerable and receptive public. Jane was fined £5 and given three years good behaviour. *Ibid.* pp.323–324.
2. Lenkiewicz, Rebecca, *Jane Wenham: The Witch of Walkern*, (2015) p.94.

Index